The Goose Hunter

The Ultimate Goose-Hunting Season

By Dennis Hunt

Suggested retail **$19.95**

By Dennis Hunt

May 1997

TABLE OF CONTENTS

About the Author

Dennis Hunt is a professional goose hunter, author, video producer and seminar speaker. He has been hunting geese for over 30 years. Chasing and studying geese is his life. There may be a better goose hunter out there, but nobody has observed or studied more geese than Dennis Hunt. Mr. Hunt is the author of three other books on goose hunting:

    1994–The Science of Snow Goose Hunting
    1995–Goose Hunting: Improving Your Skills
    1996–Out-Finessing The Geese

In 1996, Dennis Hunt produced the video The Science of Goose Hunting.

Dennis would like to hear from you if you have any questions about geese or goose hunting. He can be reached at:

Box 131235, St. Paul MN 55113
Phone: 612-649-0023 or 218-847-5147
Fax: 612-644-3653

If you would like to purchase any of Dennis Hunt's previous books or the video, see page 134 of this book for information.

Contributing Photography: Bill Marchel

Book layout and design, illustrations: Teresa Marrone

Dennis Hunt would like to acknowledge the following companies who have made this book possible through their contributions and assistance:

Federal Cartridge Co.
Higdon Motion Decoy Co.
Rice Lake Products Co.
Brigade Quartermaster–
    ASAT Camouflage
Kaufman of Canada–Sorel Boots
Hunting Classics–Over-The-Boot
    Waders
Bobby Hale and Third Coast
    Outfitters
Kaskattama Safari Adventures
    Ltd. (Kaska Goose Camp)
Cattleman's Motel & Restaurant,
    Bay City, Texas
North Wind Decoy Co.

Outlaw Decoy Co.
Sportsmax LLC
Sports Rap Systems–Gun Raps
Otter Sleds
Norwesco
Spence Marine–Water Scout
Dymond Hunting Lodge,
    Churchill, Manitoba
Scheels All Sports
Flambeau Decoy Co.

Thanks also goes to:
George Gage, Rick Julian and
Jack Crabtree – U.S. Fish and
Wildlife Service

Introduction

In 1996, I was fully retired and decided to chase geese and catch fish the rest of my life. I knew where I could catch fish in Minnesota and where I could chase geese in southern Manitoba and Nebraska. However, I wanted to chase geese from September 1 through March 10. Those are the legal guidelines that you can hunt waterfowl in North America and I wanted to do it.

I had planned to hunt in southern Manitoba the whole month of October with my many friends, and I had a guide service in Nebraska where I would be from February 8 through March 10 for the late-season snow goose hunt. I needed some place to hunt in northern Manitoba during the month of September, and a place to hunt in Texas during the months of November, December and January.

I have written three books on goose hunting and produced a video on goose hunting. In 1995, I gave 81 goose-hunting seminars at sports shows, Game Fairs and various sporting goods stores in several states. I talked to over 22,000 goose hunters at these events. Because of my following and expertise at decoying geese, I was invited to go to the only two goose hunting camps in northern Manitoba, Kaskattama Safari Adventures (Kaska Goose Camp) and Dymond Hunting Lodge. Both camps are on Hudson Bay, with Dymond being 25 miles north of Churchill and Kaska 180 miles south of Churchill.

With commitments to being in southern and northern Manitoba as well as Nebraska, I was looking forward to getting a commitment with someone in Texas. I wrote to Bobby Hale at Third Coast Outfitters in Bay City, Texas, and this was the best letter I ever wrote. I had inquired about working as a goose guide for 90 days and my offer was accepted by Third Coast Outfitters.

With God willing and some cooperation from the weather, I would be able to hunt for 185 days out of a possible 191. I was physically and mentally prepared, and being born a little crazy, I was ready to give it a try. I would be able to hunt in the four different regions while studying the geese and making comparisons to hunting terrains, styles of goose hunting and patterns/harvests of geese. I would be able to obtain plenty of information for more goose hunting books and videos, as well as lots of stories to tell the audiences at my many goose hunting seminars. I was all pumped up when I completed my plans for the long and tough trip that would take me over 3,000 miles, and take up almost seven months of my life. I was ready to go hunting.

Planning the Trip

If you ever decide, as I did in 1996, to make a goose-hunting trip that will start on August 26 and end on March 10, you are in for some heavy planning. Nothing can be overlooked and you must be prepared both mentally and physically. In preparation for an epic trip like this, you should have a complete physical and make a trip to your friendly dentist. You will be gone 185 days and need to be prepared for the worst. You will come close to getting the "burnt out syndrome" and be within inches of becoming insane. To be crazy before you make this trip would help! Here are some things you have to be prepared for:

Sickness: Viruses, stomach problems, exhaustion, frostbite and hypothermia are all possibilities.

Attacks by: Insects or bugs, snakes, fire ants, wild animals (i.e. polar or brown bears), wild hogs, alligators, etc.

Injuries that might occur: Heart attack, broken limbs, vehicle accidents, drowning, allergy or rash outbreaks, etc.

Any of the above could happen and you have to be aware of the possibilities. If you are a diabetic or taking any special medication, make it known to your friends in hunting camp.

When sorting out your equipment for this trip, you must take into consideration that you will be hunting on the tundra where it could get extremely cold; you will be hunting in southern Manitoba where you could experience normal hunting conditions but it could snow; and you will be hunting in south Texas where it might be 85 one day with a high of 25 the next day. Hunting in southern Nebraska in February and early March will be unpredictable. Lows of minus 10 to 30 above will be the range, and it might only be a high of 20 but it could be 70. When the south wind prevails, it will be warm. When a cold front comes through, the temperatures will drop, the water might freeze and the geese could fly back to Kansas. My advice is, you can never have enough warm clothes on a hunting trip.

I made two separate trips to the hunting camps in northern Manitoba. On each trip, I took:

Shells: One case of Federal 12-gauge.

Guns: Two 12-gauge shotguns in gunwrap case with gun cleaning supply kit.

Clothing: In addition to the usual clothes needed for a two-week trip, I took the following: one pair of Sorel rubber boots; one pair of Sorel lined boots; one pair of over-the-boot waders by Hunting Classics; two hunting outfits by Brigade Quartermaster and four assorted hats/caps.

Miscellaneous: Camera or cam-corder with back-up film and batteries; alarm clock.

No decoys or other hunting equipment were necessary because I flew from Winnipeg into the camps. At Dymond and Kaska hunting camps, they will purchase any shells and/or beverages and have them waiting for you. *Beware*—bring your cans of bug spray when going into Manitoba!

After returning from northern Manitoba, I took a couple of days off and returned to St. Paul, Minnesota where I gathered up my equipment trailer that is full of hunting equipment and decoys. I had over 4,100 quality decoys in my 16'x8' HH and W cargo trailer. The reason for so many decoys? We were going to have as many as four hunting parties in southern Manitoba. I would be in southern Manitoba for 30 days and this is the list of things that I brought along:

Shells: Three cases of Federal (one case of 10-gauge and two cases of 12-gauge).

Guns: Two 12-gauge and one 10-gauge.

Dennis Hunt with his Hunting Classic over-the-boot waders. These are essential when hunting in wet conditions; you just slip the waders over your boots and hunt in comfort. They are made from Cordura and weigh almost nothing.

Clothing: I took enough clothes for 30 days; eight hunting outfits from Brigade Quartermaster with 12 assorted caps/hats; one pair of Hunting Classic over-the-boot waders (see the photo at left); two pairs of Sorel hunting boots and one pair of Sorel rubber boots.

Miscellaneous: alarm clock; assorted waterfowl calls; spare trailer tire; tool box, tow chain and bumper jack; first-aid kit; camcorder, camera, extra film and batteries; coolers and refreezable ice packs; cellular phone.

In addition to the decoys, I had portable blinds, a fake poly pond, Otter small and medium-sized sleds for duck hunting, Sports-Rap Gun Wrap, Sportsmax 5-foot plastic sleds, Sportsmax Killer Kites, Flagman Flags and pole kites, Higdon Motion Cam with 12-volt battery and charger, and my new Water Scout 14-foot foam-filled duck boat from Spence Marine. You can see that I need a good equipment trailer!

One of Dennis Hunt's utility trailers for goose decoys and a duck boat are just some of the things you need while hunting geese and ducks in southern Manitoba.

My equipment list for Texas wasn't quite as extensive as that for southern Manitoba. I needed clothes for three months and seven cases of Federal shells. My Classic over-the-boot waders and Sorel rubber boots were mighty necessary because of the wet conditions in Texas. I took along 12 different hunting outfits from Brigade Quartermaster, but I used only four of them. The weather in south Texas is warm, warm and warmer, and I never had to use my sub-zero clothes in Texas.

I took two 12-gauge and one 10-gauge shotguns with me to Texas. Third Coast Outfitters furnished the decoys that were to be used. However, I brought along 250 North Wind windsocks which were needed. I also brought eight Sportsmax 5' plastic sleds which turned out to be very popular. The hunter/clients enjoyed laying in the dry sleds instead of in the wet, muddy soil. Flagman flags were taken along and they sure fooled the geese. The same for the Sportsmax Killer Kites, which attracted lots of geese. I took along 24 North Wind hovering decoys which created additional movement as well as shielding the hunters from the view of the geese and ducks. I had 72 Outlaw Canada silhouettes and they fooled lots of specks and small Canadas. I shot 42 specks in 42 days by using the silhouettes in my spreads. (The limit is one per day for both specklebelly and Canada goose in Texas.)

The decoy numbers I used in southern Nebraska were less than in southern Manitoba. I left my Canada silhouettes behind, as well as my 1,000 full-body snow goose decoys. We used shells and North Wind windsocks. The winds blow hard in Nebraska in February and March, and the windsocks looked great. I took all 20 of my Sportsmax 5' plastic sleds because I have a guide service that employs four other guides who take out four hunter/clients. The sleds are a life saver because of the water and mud in the flooded corn fields. Without the sleds, we might have gotten washed away! The Hunting Classic over-the-boot waders and the Sorel rubber boots are a must if you hunt in Nebraska in February. I also took along an extra rain suit to Nebraska because of the wet conditions. Otherwise, the hunting clothes I used in Nebraska were the same as the ones I used in southern Manitoba.

During the Nebraska leg of the trip, I used my last three cases of Federal shells; overall, I averaged 20 shells per day for the 185-day hunting trip. I still haven't had a Federal shotgun shell malfunction in 31 years of hunting.

We had two boats with us in Nebraska. We took the Outlaw Ducker, the best large duck boat I have ever used, and my Water Scout from Spence

Some of the author's supply of ammunition for the 1996 season. Dennis started the long trip with 15 cases of Federal shells in 10- and 12-gauge, and still ended up purchasing more in Nebraska. Dennis Hunt has yet to have a Federal shell malfunction in 31 years of hunting, and that is a lot of Federal shells!

Marine. This is the best small duck boat I have ever entered. The reason for the boats was the chance of putting out Higdon floaters in deeper and larger bodies of water. As it turned out, the boats weren't necessary.

Northern Manitoba

I drove my 1990 Ford F-150 4x4 up to Winnipeg, Manitoba on Monday, August 26, 1996. I parked the truck at the airport and boarded a Calm Air prop jet for Gillam, Manitoba. From Gillam, I was to board a commuter 1966 Islander and fly to Kaskattama Safari Adventures Ltd. (Kaska Goose Camp). This was the start of my long and tough hunting trip that would also take me to Dymond Hunting Lodge at Churchill,

Calm Air, a commercial jet service, flew Dennis Hunt from Winnipeg, Manitoba to Gillam, Manitoba, where he took a charter flight to Kaska Goose Camp. Dennis flew Calm Air a few weeks later to Dymond Hunting Camp.

Manitoba. From Dymond, I would hunt geese and ducks in southern Manitoba until October 28, 1996. I would travel out of Manitoba to St. Paul, Minnesota to rest for a few days, and load and unload goose hunting equipment before heading to south Texas until February 3, 1997, I would leave Texas and go back to St. Paul and pick up most of my decoys, then head for the late-season snow goose hunt in Nebraska. That would last until March 10, which is the last legal day of waterfowl hunting under the federal guidelines.

The flight to Gillam was smooth and took two hours. There was a 30-minute wait for one of the commuter passengers, a native that would be

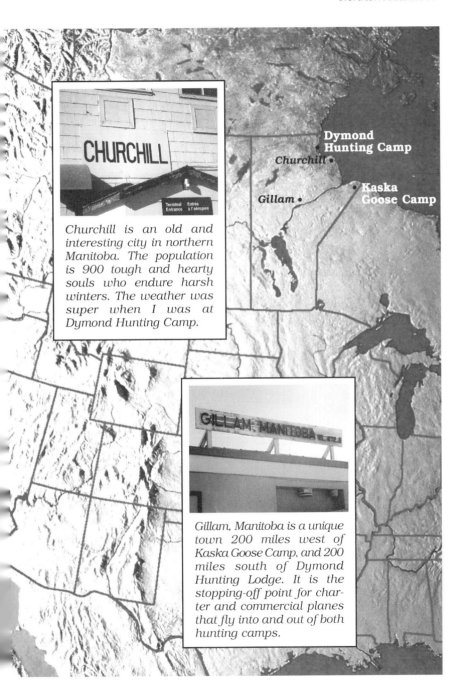

CHURCHILL

Terminal Entrance / Entrée à l'aérogare

Dymond Hunting Camp

Churchill

Gillam

Kaska Goose Camp

Churchill is an old and interesting city in northern Manitoba. The population is 900 tough and hearty souls who endure harsh winters. The weather was super when I was at Dymond Hunting Camp.

GILLAM, MANITOBA

Gillam, Manitoba is a unique town 200 miles west of Kaska Goose Camp, and 200 miles south of Dymond Hunting Lodge. It is the stopping-off point for charter and commercial planes that fly into and out of both hunting camps.

You will encounter this sign as you arrive at Kaskattama Safari Camp. This sign is located at the end of the 3,000' airstrip where your charter plane lands. Kaska Goose Camp is 200 miles from the nearest town, and is located on Hudson Bay.

picking and cleaning waterfowl at Kaska. After he arrived, we took off and flew the 200 miles east to Kaska. The plane was old but the flight was effortless as we flew down the coast of Hudson Bay en route to Kaska. We had the opportunity to see seven polar bears between York Factory and Kaska. They were wandering down the shoreline looking for a free meal.

We landed at Kaska on the 3,000' gravel airstrip. We were met there by Charlie Taylor, the camp manager and minority stockholder. Charlie is in his early 60s and is a veteran camp manager. He showed me to the staff quarters, the guest quarters, the dining facilities and repair/storage buildings. Kaska Goose Camp is 200 miles from the nearest town and all of the materials had to be flown into Kaska to build the facilities. They have an eight-man guest house that was built in 1994, and a second eight-man guest house that was erected in 1995. Kaska's ultra-fine facilities might be compared to any Marriott. The food at the Marriott is not as good as that at Kaska; nothing could be! Kaska will erect a new dining facility in 1997, and they might

Two of the tame Canada geese, Dumb and Dumber, are waiting for a free meal outside the Kaska Kitchen. The geese flew into Kaska in August and made themselves at home. You could touch and scratch the geese, just like the cat in the picture.

have the finest hunting camp in the world.

My duties at Kaska would be to clean, separate and install the decoys at the 16 goose-hunting blinds. This would have to be done by August 31 because the goose season started on September 1. There were over 2,000 decoys in the inventory, and some were old and obsolete. Over the years, most of the stockholders would purchase decoys and bring them to Kaska on their annual goose-hunting trip. There was a huge pile to sort through and separate. I picked out some full-body decoys that were made by Herters. There were over 500 of these in Canada, snow and blue goose patterns. To complement the full-body decoys, I found 12 dozen North Wind windsocks in Canada and snow patterns.

Kaska has eight blinds on the east end of the

Dennis Hunt with one of the decoy spreads at Kaska Goose Camp. Note the tundra terrain, with Hudson Bay in the background. Dennis was wearing his Brigade Quartermaster camouflage.

camp and eight on the west end. I would set up 12 full-body Canada and eight Canada windsocks along with 12 full-body snow and 8 snow windsocks on each blind. The driftwood blinds would be in the middle of each spread, and the decoys were set in rich vegetation consisting of grass, clover, etc. This is what the geese would be feeding on, along with berries and kelp weed.

Tricking geese by using the decoy system is my strong suit. Charlie Taylor was concerned about his clients/hunters getting as many shooting opportunities as possible in 1996. That is why he invited me to come to Kaska Goose Camp. As it turned out, after 14 days at Kaska, almost everyone shot their limits of eight birds per day (of which only five could be Canada geese). I was satisfied with my efforts of erecting the decoy spreads and repairing the blinds.

The daily routine at Kaska is:

1. Wake at 5 a.m.

2. Breakfast at 5:30.

3. Depart for your hunting destination at 6:15 via all-terrain vehicles. Two drivers would take eight hunters and equipment to their blinds.

4. Hunters would be in their blinds and would hunt from 6:45 to 11:30 a.m. The driver would pick up the hunters at 11:30 to enjoy a great lunch. If the hunters wanted to stay, a lunch would be provided.

5. After lunch, hunters would decide what time to go back out to hunt. Some would want to nap and that had to be decided. Hunters would usually go back out and hunt from 3:30 to 7:30 when the driver would come back out and pick the hunters up.

6. A four-star dinner would be served at 8:15 by Christine Quinlan, the chef *par excellence.*

7. Most hunters would have a libation and retire at 9:30 to be ready to do it all over again.

Dennis Hunt and Jan Collins from the Manitoba Department of Tourism. Limits are not guaranteed at Kaska, but are easy to obtain.

The patterns of the geese and the results of the harvests will be told later in this book. However, I want to talk about tundra hunting and what a great trip it was.

Dennis Hunt in these two photos is showing off nice harvests of geese taken at Kaska. As you can see from the photos, a variety of clothing is needed when you are hunting geese and ducks in Manitoba, because weather and the temperatures are not predictable.

There are only one in 100,000 goose hunters that know what it is like to hunt on Hudson Bay or an area similar to it. I was one of those 100,000 naive goose hunters that arrived at Kaska. The weather in early September at Kaska can be pleasant, but it can get nasty. Eleven of the 14 days, the temperature was in the 70's. A front came thru on September 2 and it got cold with the temperature dropping to a high of 48. This lasted only three days and things got back to normal. You have to have warm clothing along because you could get snow anytime. I wasn't bothered by the cold; I simply put a heavier hunting jacket on and got on with the business of hunting geese.

The Kaska Camp is on the Kaskattama River and is two miles from the coast of Hudson Bay. On the Hudson Bay, there are a lot of rocks and mud as the tide comes and goes twice a day. The tide washes kelp weed into shore and the Canada geese will eat that weed as the tide goes out. When the tide is in, the Canada geese will be feeding on grass or berries on the eksters. This is a high ridge of land that is usually 200 yards wide, followed by a low area of land and another ekster. The eksters were created by the glaciers millions of years ago. Along the coast, the ground is almost barren. As you go further inland, there are small berry bushes that are two to three feet tall. Further inland, the bushes and trees become taller. The driftwood hunting blinds are sticking up on the barren land with no bushes or trees to hide them. However, the geese don't pay any attention to them because they are migrating along the coast and looking for something to eat. Geese are distracted by movement and if the blinds don't move, the geese won't flare off of them.

You have to be concerned with the mud and the

slippery conditions while you are hunting along the coast. After the tide goes out, there is a lot of mud left behind. I had my Sorel rubber boots along (made by Kaufman Footwear, 1-800-265-2760), and my leather Sorel boots accompanied by a pair of over-the-boot waders (made by Hunting Classics at Tallapoosa, Georgia (770-574-961).

The waders weigh less than two pounds and come with suspenders. You slip them over any boot and your feet are dry. There are a couple of blinds on the east end of Kaska that are next to a branch of the Kaskattama River. When you flare a goose that has been shot, it may land on the other side of the river. To get there, Kaska has provided a 12' aluminum boat that you can row across 100 yards to get to your goose. However, the banks of this river are very muddy and treacherous. Put your rubber boots on! Also, if hunting all day on the east end, watch the

These geese were shot by two hunters out of Kaska Goose Camp. When the tide comes in on the Hudson Bay, the Canada geese are forced to fly on the shoreline and over the driftwood blinds. When the tide goes out, the geese go out and feed on the kelp weed that the waves wash in.

tide because it could interfere with your plans... but it can also help you, if you take advantage of it. I met two e x c e l l e n t hunters from W e s t l a k e , Ohio who would go out on the shoreline and lay in the mud and rocks and kill Canada geese. When the tide would go out, the Canadas would begin looking for the kelp weed. Don and Ben Kaatz would lay in their c a m o u f l a g e outfits and wait for the

Donald Kaatz from Westlake, Ohio and the author admire a harvest of Canada geese. Kaatz was one of the most talented hunters that Dennis encountered while in northern Manitoba. Also in the picture are two tame Canada geese that were adopted at Kaska and acted like one of the gang!

geese to fly over. They would get their limit of five almost every day while at Kaska.

While hunting the eksters at Kaska, you have to beware of the berry bushes. There are black, goose, blue, fire etc. berry bushes and the thorns on some of these branches are sharp and will cut your skin or hunting outfits. Wear a pair of cotton gloves while hunting the eksters. There is also some poison ivy that lurks within these berry bushes. If you are allergic to any poison bushes or vines, take precautions.

The wild animals at Kaska are few. Once a year you may see some timber wolves, but they have never bothered anyone. The polar bear is of great concern. However, you are always on the lookout for them but you will never see one. They don't migrate south out of Churchill because they are waiting for the Hudson Bay to freeze so they can out on the ice and go seal hunting. A polar bear could weigh up to 1,600 pounds, stand 12 feet tall and run up to 40 miles per hour.

I took a helicopter ride up the coast to York Factory to see how many snow geese were staging there. We left at 3 p.m. for the 100-mile trip north. We flew along the coast and we saw a spectacular sight. There was a beluga whale that had died and was washed ashore. We saw the whale from the helicopter, 300 yards in the air. Eating lunch on the whale were nine polar bears. This was a scary sight.

There was a family of brown bears near the camp at Kaska. The bears had been feeding on berries until the bird pluckers started cleaning geese. The bird pluckers would clean the geese and ducks in their bird house. After they were done with

Delbert Wavey, the bird picker champion, plucks some birds at Kaska Goose Camp. This is a tough way to make a living!

The bird picking facility at Kaska Goose Camp. Delbert Wavey and Raymond Saunders held down the fort and presided over this facility. With 16 clients and some guests that were hunting daily, picking/plucking over 100 birds a day was a common occurrence. This job isn't for everyone!

the birds, they would take the guts and feathers and dump them into a huge sand pit which was near the home of the brown bears. Within the family of bears was the daddy bear who weighed almost 800 pounds. The mama bear weighed almost 600 pounds and the baby bear weighed 250. The bird pluckers would dump the remains into the huge hole within the sand pit and the daddy bear would enter the pit and eat for several hours. The mama and baby bear would wait for their turn in the pit while the daddy bear gorged himself. Feathers would fly and all you could see of that bear would be the top of his head. After several hours, papa bear would exit the pit and walk to the Kaskattama River to get a drink. Mama bear would take her turn while the baby bear waited for crumbs. If mama bear exited before papa got back, the baby bear would get into the pit for a goose dinner. Otherwise, he would have to settle for the berries to eat. Everyone at the camp was aware of the brown bears, but the bears didn't bother anyone.

When you travel to different hunting camps you will encounter some great goose hunters and super sportsman. A couple come to mind that I will never forget. Outside of the Kaatz brothers from Ohio, there was Kevin Vaughan from Sioux City, Iowa. Kevin is a tenacious hunter and a super shot. He would stay out in his blind from dawn to dusk and would always bring in his limit.

Kevin is a minority stockholder in Kaska and he bought along seven of his best customers who also were good goose hunters. Another minority stockholder in Kaska and super hunter was Ted Northam from Winnipeg, Manitoba. He was along with a majority Kaska stockholder, Tom Smith from St. Bonifacius, Minnesota.

I hunted with Northam and Smith one morning and we shot our limit of 24 geese before 10 a.m. Tom Smith is one of the best shots I have ever had the pleasure of hunting with.

Kaska Goose Camp was a great experience, and 14 days of the greatest hunting with super accommodations. I would recommend it. For more information about Kaska write:

Charlie Taylor
170 Harbison Avenue West
Winnipeg, Manitoba R2L 0A4 (Canada)
Phone: 204-667-1611

I left Kaska Goose Camp on a high note after experiencing 14 great days. Eight of us boarded the chartered prop-jet at the Kaska runway as eight new hunters got off. We were headed for Winnipeg where we were going to get back to civilization. I would drive back to St. Paul and then turn around, go back to Winnipeg and board another plane for Churchill and Dymond Hunting Lodge.

On September 16, 1997, I boarded a Calm Air jet to Churchill with a stop at Gillam, Manitoba. After arriving at Churchill, we were met by Doug Webber, the owner of Dymond Hunting Lodge, and Stewart Webber (no relation), Dymond's manager. Doug piloted the float plane that took us north 25 miles to the camp, which is on Hudson Bay.

These four hunters from Rockford, Illinois are about to enter the float plane back to Churchill and to civilization after hunting at Dymond Hunting Lodge. The plane is piloted by Doug Webber, owner of Dymond Hunting Lodge.

Stewart Webber showed us to our accommodations, a beautiful guest house that was home for 16 of us. This building can be compared to a Marriott as could the lodges at Kaska. The cooking is done by Helen Webber and is the equal to Kaska. You could stay at either camp, work and hunt hard for 14 days and go home with 14 more pounds on you. They really feed

The new guest facility at Dymond Hunting Lodge, 25 miles north of Churchill, Manitoba. The guest and dining facilities at both Dymond and Kaska can compare to any Marriott. Both materials and workers must be flown into these camps.

you well at the goose camps in northern Manitoba!

Dymond uses driftwood blinds as does Kaska. Dymond has a blind built within 300 yards of the camp call Hamburger Hill. When the wind is from the correct direction, migrating geese will fly down the shoreline and then cut the corner and fly over Hamburger Hill. There is a spread of decoys on

The staff quarters at Dymond Hunting Lodge. There were two cooks/waitresses, the manager (Stewart Webber), a bird picker, and three Cree guides working at Dymond. Doug Webber, the owner, worked between the hunting and fishing camps that Dymond operates.

Dennis Hunt with a limit of geese shot at Dymond Hunting Lodge. The decoys were set up on one of the eksters, which is higher ground created by ancient glaciers. Note the berry bushes that grow on the eksters, as well as the short trees whose growth is governed by the strong winds on the tundra.

the hill to attract the geese and the shooting is fantastic. The migration of geese was on and there was a continuous stream of families of geese that were flying over Hamburger Hill for two weeks. There were Ross, snows, blues and three different styles of Canada geese. We could tell the season was coming to an end because there was a good migration of swans flying over. Swans are protected in the province of Manitoba. Ducks were scarce because most of them had already migrated through the area and were heading south and west.

The agenda for hunting at Dymond is similar to Kaska. After a great breakfast, they take you out and you have the choice of staying there all day or being picked up at 11:30 and going back to camp to eat lunch and rest.

I hit it lucky at both northern Manitoba hunting camps. I got into the migrations of geese and had some super hunting at both camps. I shot over 200 geese in northern Manitoba with the limits being eight per day. Most of the hunters sign over their harvested geese and the local natives will take them.

A nice harvest of snows and Canada geese in northern Manitoba. The large Canadas weigh 10 to 12 pounds; most of the snows are mature birds that seemed unaware of the Manitoba hunting season.

The possession limit in Manitoba was 32, so if you are going to stay within the law, you have to give away any over the legal limit. The conservation officers have an obligation to check out each camp annually but I never did see them. They came at Kaska while I was taking a nap and they arrived at Dymond one day before I arrived.

The weather at Churchill set some records in September. Usually, you would expect to run into some snow but they had 19 consecutive days that were over 70 degrees. I took along a Brigade Quartermaster lined hunting outfit that was good for 40 below zero and I found myself hunting without a shirt on several afternoons. You have to remember to bring along a can of bug spray because the flies and bugs can get thick.

There is little danger from wild animals at Dymond outside of the polar bears. They wander down the coast more often than Kaska waiting for the water to freeze on Hudson Bay. The Fish and Wildlife Service has a headquarters building in Churchill with a polar bear jail. If a polar bear comes close to camp, the conservation officers will come with a crew and a helicopter and tranquilize the bear and haul him off to jail. They hold them there until the bay is frozen in November, and then release them.

Dymond Hunting Lodge is a unique camp because of the facilities and the beauty. They offer you the chance to hunt ptarmigan which are close to the camp, or you can hire them to take you hunting for caribou or fishing for northern pike, arctic grayling, brook trout, lake trout or walleye. I would recommend Dymond Hunting Lodge to everyone, as I would Kaska. As of this writing, I have been the first goose hunter to visit both camps in the same year and I want to thank God for the opportunity. The short hunting seasons (less than 28 days) at each camp and the economics make it tough to get to both camps in the same season.

To book a hunt at Dymond Hunting Lodge, write:
Stewart Webber or Doug Webber
P.O. Box 304
Churchill, Manitoba R0B 0E0 (Canada)
Toll-free phone: 800-665-0476
Phone: 204-675-2583

Southern Manitoba

I arrived at the Winnipeg airport from Churchill and drove back to St. Paul, Minnesota. I would stay there for two days, then pack up the rest of my hunting equipment for my goose hunting stay in southern Manitoba which would last until October 28. That is the usual date when things get frozen up and the ducks and geese leave and migrate south.

The waterfowl season for non-Canadians would begin on September 30 and I wanted to get there early so I could scout the area. I had a lot of friends that would join me over the next 30 days and I wanted to show them a good goose hunt.

I arrived in southern Manitoba on Friday and that left me with two full days to find the geese, find out what they were feeding on and where, and try to figure out their patterns. The two full days would give me plenty of time. I would be hunting predominantly snow geese and I knew the areas well because I have hunted this spot for over 20 years. I am not going to mention the names of any towns because I don't want too much company in my hunting area! I will mention that I hunt close to the North Dakota border and I am east of Boissevain and south of Brandon.

The first migration of snows and blues usually arrive in my area near the 15th of September. There are two migrations of them, and the second migration will come through around October 8. The geese stay around until October 15 and then fly south and settle on the border of North Dakota. Most of these geese will stay on the Manitoba side. Some might fly into North Dakota and find a roost pond but will fly north to feed in Manitoba. They do this because of the hunting pressure. Between October 15 and October 25, in North Dakota, there is intense

Can you spot the calf moose in this picture? He was later seen walking around in the author's decoy spread in southern Manitoba.

hunting pressure compared to Manitoba. The geese and the ducks know this.

In my hunting area, we try to keep the hunting pressure off the geese.

We try not to hunt the same flocks two days in a row. The goose hunting season ends at 12 noon the first 11 days of the season and that helps. The season changes to all-day hunting the second Saturday of the season and the disposition of the geese will change. We hunt in an area where there might be eight roost ponds where the geese will stay at night. These are on private lands and they are within five miles of the motel where we stay. This is very convenient and we want to keep it that way. If we shoot the birds off the roost ponds and they leave the area, we will have to leave the area or drive another 25 miles to where the geese have gone. We want the geese to stay around because geese attract geese.

The terrain in southern Manitoba is similar to that in northern North Dakota. The land is flat in most

This is the typical terrain in southern Manitoba. The land is flat and easy to drive a vehicle onto. The bale of straw in the background will make a natural blind.

Tommy Schneider, Tom Gustafson, Bobby Lester and Kurt Graff from Minneapolis admire the nice harvest of ducks and geese taken while hunting in southern Manitoba with Dennis Hunt.

areas and there are small lakes and ponds. Southern Manitoba is the duck factory of North America and this was verified in 1996. We sure saw a lot of ducks and everyone in my hunting parties went home with their limit of 12 ducks. If you go east to west, starting with highway 75 that goes into Winnipeg and then go over to Saskatchewan, the land is the same from the North Dakota border and 40 miles north. There are areas within this tract that don't have much water and you won't have many ducks or geese. However, the areas within that do have water to hold the waterfowl are great hunting spots.

The crops that attract geese are barley, peas, corn and wheat. The prices on these crops have been high the past three years so there has been a lot of barley and wheat grown. You don't see many pea fields, but if you do, they will attract lots of geese. Landowners are growing more corn because they have more

cattle and the price of corn has been high. Corn fields attract lots of geese and I saw more corn grown in Manitoba in 1996 than in previous years. But there are also other crops grown in Manitoba that geese don't eat, so don't bother looking for the geese in these fields: canola, flax, sunflowers and alfalfa.

The author is in the top photo with Doctors: John Brown, Jim Brown, John Lamni, and John Sargent from Minnesota. They shot 36 mallards and three geese in 45 minutes while hunting in southern Manitoba. The coolers in the bottom picture are full of ducks and geese; this was their best hunting trip ever!

Weather in southern Manitoba is comparable to that of Grand Forks, North Dakota. It is usually reliable until October 15 and after that date, anything can happen. We had 3" of snow on October 2 and 4" on October 17. The first snowfall lasted two days, and the second snowfall lasted three days before it melted.

The species of geese that migrate through southern Manitoba are: snows, blues, a few Ross, a few white fronts, small Canadas and medium-sized Canadas. The majority of the medium-sized Canadas do not migrate through until late in October. Most of them will stay at the Oak Hammock area, north of Winnipeg. They stay there until the waters freeze

Dennis Hunt with a harvest of snows, blues, Canadas and specks that were shot in southern Manitoba by Hunt and his friends. Hunting parties of four would bring in 15 to 32 consistently.

and then leave together. Some will filter through our area and stop for a day or two. We shot 14 white fronts in 1996 and this was unusual. We usually shoot five to 10 Ross geese and we shot eight in 1996 in 28 days of hunting. The majority of the geese we kill are snows, blues and small Canadas.

There are no serious hazards that you have to beware of in southern Manitoba. There are lots of deer running across the roads as you travel to your field in the morning that you will have to watch out for. The whitetail deer are called "jumpers" in Manitoba. You will encounter muddy conditions on some prairie roads and you might bring along a tow chain in case your vehicle slides off any road. A truck with 4x4 is almost a must, especially if the conditions are wet. There are wild animals in southern Manitoba. However, the wolves, coyotes, fox and bears are seldom seen during waterfowl season. The only thing that will attack you is the flies. Bring along that can of bug spray!

When you are hunting geese in southern Manitoba, you will need normal hunting equipment. This is what you would need (party of 4):

General:
- 4x4 truck with jumper cables and tow chain
- Trailer for the decoys with spare tire and bumper jack

Decoys:
- 144 Higdon full bodies in snow, with 48 Convertadecoy sleeves to convert your white decoys to brown for Canadas

Al Murphy, Ed Huffstetler and Jeff Rokeh are getting their straw ready for the opening of goose hunting season in southern Manitoba. The straw is used to cover the hunters who lay in fields near the decoys. The geese see the straw, but not the hunters.

Chuck Glaser, Jr., Wayne and Larry Hoffstrom, and Chuck Glaser, Sr. from Minnesota are admiring the geese they fooled with decoys in southern Manitoba. Eight hunters shot 48 geese and 45 mallards in three hours, shooting over 400 rounds of shells.

- 288 North Wind windsocks in snow and blue. I use the Canada body with the white head.
- 144 Outlaw snow and 72 Outlaw Canada silhouettes if you have to be mobile
- 6 Flagman flags
- 2 "killer kites" or Outlaw kites
- 12 duck decoys.

Hunting Equipment:

- 4 Sportsmax 5' plastic sleds to lay in and haul equipment
- 12 burlap sacks to use to fill up with straw from the fields
- 4 burlap stake blinds
- 4 sheets of earth-tone camouflage
- 4 sheets of white camouflage or white sheets in case of snow

Personal Equipment:
- 1 shotgun and 1 back-up shotgun
- 10 boxes Federal shells (6 for geese, 3 for ducks, 1 for sharptail)
- 1 gun cleaning supply kit
- 1 cellular phone in case of accidents
- 1 first-aid kit
- 1 alarm clock
- Necessary clothes for the trip
- 1 pair of Hunting Classic over-the-boot waders
- 1 pair of Sorel rubber boots
- 2 pair of Sorel hunting boots
- Necessary hunting clothes for warm and cold conditions
- Camera or cam-corder with back up film and batteries.
- Coolers and ice packs
- Equipment to clean and preserve the game

If you are going to hunt in southern Manitoba for the first time, get up there in early summer, check

This group of hunters from Minneapolis and Fargo shot over 70 geese while hunting in southern Manitoba. Kurt Knoff, second from the left, enjoys his victory cigar.

the area out, make some arrangements to hunt on private land and get a motel reservation.

Hunting in southern Manitoba is easy in comparison to northern Manitoba, Texas and southern Nebraska in the spring. During normal conditions, you will have your trailer hitched to your 4x4 and leave the motel at 5 a.m. You will drive three to five miles right onto the field in which you will be hunting. Everyone pitches in to unload and set up the decoys and establish the blinds. You will be finished with the work in less than 90 minutes and sitting in your blind with a cup of coffee waiting for the first mallard or goose to fly. It is unusual to get heavy rainfall, which will prohibit you from driving onto the field. When that happens, you will be glad you have the Sportsmax 5' plastic sleds along to haul out your decoys and provide a dry place for you to lay while you are waiting for geese.

The author in the background with Terry Winter and Dr. Randall Schmitt from Clinton, Iowa. They harvested this nice bunch of gadwalls and snows in southern Manitoba.

Hunting in southern Manitoba is great and I would recommend it. For more information, call Dennis Hunt at 612-649-0023 or the Manitoba Department of Tourism at 204-945-2272.

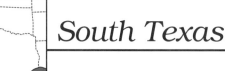

South Texas

After having my most successful goose and duck hunting trip of 20 years in southern Manitoba, I left for St. Paul, Minnesota on October 28, 1996. I was going to unload my decoy trailer, sort things out, reload some of my gear and head for south Texas. I would be working for Bobby Hale of Third Coast Outfitters at Bay City, Texas. I would guide goose hunters until February 2, then head to southern Nebraska to hunt snow geese until March 10.

I hurried with my unpacking and re-packing, repaired some of the damaged decoys and left for Texas. I stopped over in Blair, Nebraska to see my friends, George and Audrey Gage. George is a veteran Fish and Wildlife Service employee with 28 years of service, and is the wildlife manager at DeSoto National Wildlife Refuge in Missouri Valley, Iowa. This is across the Missouri River from Blair, Nebraska.

I spent the evening with the Gage's, talking about their new home, waterfowl on DeSoto Refuge at the present time and about fishing. I left early the next morning, trying to make it to the Texas border so I would be in Bay City the following afternoon. En route, I stopped at Forny Lake, an Iowa state wildlife refuge. I checked out the geese on the refuge and found about 5,000 with some getting off the refuge and heading south to migrate. The temperature was 20 above with ice forming on Forny Lake.

I left Iowa and drove down Interstate 29 with a stop at Squaw Creek National Wildlife Refuge. There had been a report of over 300,000 snows and blues holding at the refuge and I wanted to check it out. The weather was the same as that in Iowa when I stopped at Mound City, Missouri to check out Squaw

BAY CITY
CITY LIMIT
POP 18170

HISTORICAL
MARKERS
IN CITY

A great city with lots of fine people.

Bay City • Third Coast
Outfitters

Specks in south Texas. These geese are relatively easy to hunt.

Creek. It was 8:30 a.m. at the time and most of the geese had left the refuge and gone out to feed. The refuge personnel indicated that a lot of geese had left over the week-end and headed south.

From Squaw Creek, I drove to Leavenworth, Kansas to check out the amount of snow geese in that area. The power plant on the river will keep the water open all winter and will hold over 100,000 snows and blues until spring time. But the stop in Leavenworth turned out to be a waste of time. I found only 2,500 snow geese that were scattered around the various farmlands. The majority of geese had not migrated into the area for the winter.

I left Kansas and headed down to Flint Hills National Refuge to check out the numbers of geese near Hartford, Kansas. This is a different hunting area, where most of the goose hunters are gung ho over Canada geese. They tie up the prime farmlands and hunt only Canada geese and deer. The snow goose hunter is shafted because there is a shortage of places to hunt. The local goose hunters call the snow geese "sky carp." There were 250,000 snows resting on the reservoir near Flint Hills Refuge. I took a few pictures of the blotch of white in the water and headed towards the state of Oklahoma. I was to meet three police officers for dinner in Norman, Oklahoma and then stop in Ardmore, Oklahoma for the evening.

A good place to kick your boots off!

I left Oklahoma early the next morning. I drove through Dallas and then around Houston, arriving in Bay City at 2 p.m. I checked into the Cattleman's Motel, which would be my home for the next 90 days. After unpacking my belongings, I called Bobby Hale, and we made arrangements to meet for dinner. We talked over the "game plan" for the next 90 hunting days.

Nathan Patel, the owner of the Cattleman's Motel and restaurant. Nathan welcomes all hunters to Cattleman's, the headquarters for Third Coast Outfitters.

Bobby Hale, owner of Third Coast Outfitters, shows off a cross goose, snow and speck, that he called in and shot near Bay City, Texas. Bobby is the best speck caller in the world, according to my estimations.

Bobby Hale is 43 years old and a native Texan. A raw-boned man who stands 6'3" and weighs 220, he could be a tight end for the Dallas Cowboys. Bobby has owned Third Coast Out–fitters for 13 years and has four full-time and six part-time goose guides work-ing for him. The goose hunting sea-son begins the first week of November and usually lasts through mid-February in Texas. I was all pumped up!

I met Bobby Hale the next morning at 5 a.m. for a quick breakfast at the Cattleman's and headed out to see some of the proper-ties that Third Coast Outfitters leases to

Above and left: some of the mounted birds in the lobby of the Cattleman's Motel. They were shot by Bobby Hale; all have bands or collars.The bird at the very top is an 8-year-old speck.

Eagle Lake, Texas. There are more out-fitters in this area than anywhere in the world, hence there is a lot of hunting pressure and competition for the geese.

provide quality goose and duck hunting for their clients. There were over 50,000 acres that I would have to learn how to find at 5 a.m., the usual time we arrived at our daily goose hunting venues. Third Coast leases land 15 miles south, almost to the

This is a sign you will encounter near Eagle Lake, Texas. Don't mess with Texans. The penalty for trespassing on a man's land while carrying a gun is $1,000.00.

Dennis Hunt, with June Bug and Kate, looking over his duck decoys with the Gulf of Mexico in the background (below).

Gulf of Mexico. They have land west of Bay City that will take you 30 miles. From there, there are properties 15 miles north. Some ranches have 5,000 acres of agricultural lands to hunt geese on. Other farms might only have 1,000 acres of huntable land. Third Coast leases the properties annually and could pay as much as $10.00 per acre to hunt. There are other

Aransas Refuge is 80 miles west of Third Coast Outfitters. This is where the whooping cranes live in the winter. The refuge is populated with wild hogs; watch out!

available farms and ranches that Third Coast might rent on a daily fee basis, if there are geese feeding on the properties. To become an outfitter requires a huge investment and a lot of nerve. You have to secure the properties, advertise for the clients, provide good guides to provide quality goose hunts, and pray that there is some money left over at the end of the waterfowl season to turn a profit. There are also fees to pay landowners to flood some fields to provide "roost ponds" to hold the birds and liability insurance to contend with.

A flooded field in south Texas.

Geese in a maize field in south Texas. Driving on the fields in Texas is next to impossible, so you have to carry your decoys onto the field.

The agricultural lands available for the geese are in short supply. Most of the lands are leased by outfitters or hunting clubs. There is no available land to hunt on for the do-it-yourself hunter. There is also a $1,000.00 fine that would be imposed if you get caught trespassing on private property.

The geese are looking for harvested rice fields, winter wheat, rye grass and maize fields. They also settle into plowed

A rice field in south Texas, with a spread of rags to lure the birds into shooting range.

fields with small shoots of grass or weeds that have resurrected in the fields. The geese will start arriving in early October with the white fronts moving in first, followed by the snows, with the small Canadas flying in shortly after Thanksgiving. The majority of the snows were in south Texas when I arrived on November 8.

A flock of snows. There could be over 3,000,000 geese in south Texas in early November. Harvesting geese is easy in south Texas because there are lots of geese.

This was due to a severe cold front that went through Saskatchewan, Manitoba and the Dakota's. This forced all of the geese to fly south and some went straight to Texas. They overflew Nebraska because the whole state of Nebraska had their worst fall snow goose hunting season ever. Elton Benson,

Snows, blues, specks and Canadas in a south Texas rice field.

a veteran hunter and good friend of mine from Ong, Nebraska told me, "Goose hunting was so bad in 1996 that I never shot a goose."

Back to Texas! The first fields in which the geese will feed in will be the rice fields. There will be leftover grain in the field as well as shoots of the rice plant that will be starting to grow. These rice fields will be

A rice field in south Texas. This field is wet, muddy and tough to walk in. You will have a lot more success hunting geese here than in Manitoba or Nebraska; however, you had better be in good physical shape.

cleaned out by the geese by mid-December, and then the geese will move over to maize and winter

Ben Gregory, one of the best guides that Dennis Hunt has ever encountered, with the geese his clients/hunters harvested south of Bay City, Texas.

wheat fields. When the weather cools down and the geese start thinking about migrating north, they will start feeding in the rye grass fields. This usually occurs in early January when the geese become extremely vulnerable. The geese start gathering into

How would you like to lay in this field? Dennis Hunt and his clients/ hunters had to do just that many of the 90 days he hunted in Texas.

larger flocks at that time as they get ready to stage and fly north. You have to know the feeding patterns of the snow geese in Texas and speculate where they will be tomorrow. Bobby Hale is an expert at this and that is why Third Coast Outfitters has been successful with the average goose hunter getting over six geese per day, per man. That is far above the average

Dennis Hunt and Sam Gray, a 16-year-old hunter from Baytown, Texas, with a nice harvest of geese. Sam shot his first goose while hunting with the author.

Bobby Hale, owner of Third Coast Outfitters in Bay City, Texas is not only a great hunter but also a super fisherman. When Bobby passes on, the geese and fish near Bay City will have a great celebration.

of the 100 or more waterfowl outfitters in south Texas. I will talk more about the success of the Texas goose hunters later in this book.

The weather in our hunting areas was super. We were located 100 miles southwest of Houston and the weather will go below 30 only two or three times per year. It seldom snows and you will see ice on your windshield only a few

Ben Gregory, the high profile guide from Third Coast, with a client from England. You can tell by their apparel that it was a bit cool while they were hunting. The dogs, Kate and June Bug, don't seem to mind!

days. Because your body isn't used to 30 degree days, you must bring along some warm clothing. I had 12 hunting outfits from Brigade Quartermaster, but I only used four different outfits: two for cold weather and two for warm weather. I never did put on my long johns. The overnight low temperature was in the mid 60's on many occasions and we would be putting out decoys at 6 a.m. with no shirt on.

Ben Gregory from Bay City, Texas with Dave Hentosh from Maine and Johnny Lloyd from Houston with this great shoot, which includes sandhill cranes, snows and blues. With this group of "killers" is Honey, one of the most well-behaved retrievers that Dennis Hunt has ever encountered.

The high temperature during the months of October and November is always in the 70's and 80's. It will slip into the 50's a few days in December and the local residents will shiver. During the month of January, it will range between 45 and 75 for the high temperature. We were out on the Gulf of Mexico on November 17 hunting for diver ducks. We got there at 2 p.m. and left the waters at 7 p.m. We were

A porpoise that Dennis Hunt and Bobby Hale revived after two hours of staying with him. They pulled the 7-foot, 200-pound mammal out into the water with an ATV; the porpoise finally swam away and lived.

killing bluebills and redheads from a blind on one of the small islands. The temperature was 83 and we were hunting without a shirt on. The diver duck hunting can be spectacular on the coast, 10 miles east of Matagorda. Pintail hunting on the rice fields is also excellent. Third Coast has some great duck hunting spots and had some good shoots. This season started on November 16 and ended on January 19 with a seven-day recess in early December.

The things to caution you with while Texas goose hunting include: the wet and muddy fields; fire ants that will fill your arms and

John Niemann from Parma, Michigan with a 40-inch rattlesnake that Bobby Hale encountered and shot while returning to his truck.

Dennis Hunt giving the finger to a tire with 200 miles on it. Dennis had a flat while out scouting on a very muddy road. The jack would not hold up the truck and he had to walk 6.1 miles before he found help.

legs within a minute and will leave bites that take three weeks to heal; wild hogs that fear no man and eat everything; and various snakes and alligators. Luckily, snakes and alligators are rare unless you are near ponds of water while hunting ducks. The hogs will be seen early in the morning because they are night feeders. If you did wound a wild hog and he let out his distress call, the whole pack could attack your hunting group. Most hogs weigh 100 pounds, but there are stories of 550-pound boar hogs that have been shot. The water and mud in the hunting fields is another story. The hunting of geese in south Texas is difficult because of the soil conditions. The tractor and combine tire tracks

There is a feral hog in this grass. Wild hogs are everywhere in south Texas; Bobby Hale shot one that weighed over 600 pounds.

The Texas rag is the decoy that is used the most in Texas. The wind puffs them up and they look like real geese. Almost any decoy will work in south Texas. The problem is getting them out onto the field. An ATV or Sportsmax plastic sled will help. The other solution is a tough walk out.

in the fields might be 36' wide and 48' high. These fill with rain water and are difficult to walk over. It reminded me of marine boot camp many a morning.

The equipment used in south Texas goose hunting can be described as light and waterproof. Because you cannot drive onto the hunting fields, all the decoys have to transported via ATVs or a Sportsmax sled. Only a few guides own ATVs and the sleds are new to Texas goose hunters. Most carry their light decoys in ponchos or sacks. Let me tell you what you are limited to in Texas:

Decoys: North Wind windsocks, North Wind hovering windsocks, Texas rags on a wooden stake, silhouettes, kites, flags, and shells (if you have a sled).

Clothing: A white parka, windbreaker or coveralls because most hunters will lay within the decoys; a rain suit and rubber boots; waders or Hunting

John Niemann from Parma, Michigan –he's the best bird plucker in the world. What a job!

Classics over-the-boot waders. I used a pair of Sorel hunting boots that were underneath the over-the-boot waders. I was comfortable and dry from the waist down.

Cotton gloves are important to keep the fire ants off and to eliminate any chance of the geese seeing your hands. Don't leave home without cotton gloves!

Equipment: Federal shells in BBB for geese and Federal #2 for ducks; gun cleaning supply kit to clean your guns daily to get the mud off of them;

Dennis Hunt spotted this house for rent near Wharton, Texas. The price was right but he turned it down. He stayed at the Cattleman's Motel in Bay City for 90 days and was very comfortable.

Mike Kennedy on the left with his friends from Minnesota and Iowa admire a harvest of geese near Blessing, Texas.

Sportsmax 5' plastic sled to haul your gear and to lay in (Sportsmax phone # is toll free: 1-800-646-6629); miscellaneous white and burlap camouflage to cover your body and items up with; Jone's face paint, sunglasses and bug spray.

I will go into detail about the successful goose hunting in Texas later in this book and I will compare it to the other three areas I hunted on this long and tough goose hunting trip. Hunting in south Texas is great and the experience is educational. I would recommend hunting in south Texas. To book a hunt with Third Coast Outfitters, write to Bobby Hale at:

P.O. Box 1351
Bay City, Texas 77404-1351
Toll-free phone: 1-888-TX-GEESE
409-245-3071

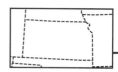

I left the State of Texas on Saturday, February 1 and arrived in southern Nebraska on Sunday morning, February 2. The state was clear of snow. However, because the temperature was in the mid-thirties, the waters were frozen. When that occurs, you won't find any ducks or geese. They have to have a place to roost safely or they will fly somewhere they can find a safe roost pond.

I drove up Kansas #81 as far as Nebraska #4 and turned west to Davenport, Nebraska. From there I went to Ong and had breakfast at the Village Inn. I have eaten there many times when I have hunted the Clay Center area in the fall. Danny serves the best meals in southern Nebraska and he usually knows if there are any geese around. I asked him that question and found that no geese had been seen yet. The season in this area opened on February 1 and runs thru February 15. Unless it warmed up, there wouldn't be a late snow season in Zone 1, which included the Ong area.

From Ong, I drove east through Fairbury and then on to Beatrice. I never saw a goose, nor did I see any open water. I was due to come back to Beatrice on the 7th of February and start guiding clients on February 8. I would have to cancel this out because there would not be a migration of geese until February 17, 1997.

I stopped at the Super 8 motel in Beatrice and confirmed my reservations for myself, my guides and my clients. I cancelled the reservations indicated that I would be making new reservations, as soon as the geese arrived. I drove back to St. Paul to get some R and R and keep an eye on the Weather Channel and the southern Nebraska weather.

Back in Minnesota, I got some well deserved rest.

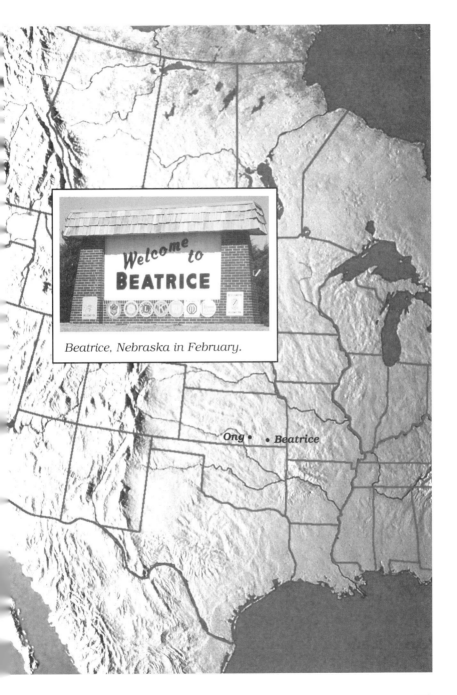

Beatrice, Nebraska in February.

I had been out in hunting camps or hunting since August 26 and I was somewhere between being burned out and insane. I needed a break.

It snowed in southern Nebraska on February 4 and that shut down the geese for another week. The manager of the Motel 8 in Beatrice called me and asked, "When are you and your hunters coming down?" I told him, "As soon as you warm up southern Nebraska!"

It finally warmed up and I left for Nebraska on February 18. That was the day that there was a significant migration of geese. I arrived in Beatrice, Nebraska around 6 pm and was met there by one of my guides. He had gotten there the day before, and had been out looking for geese and arranging for places to hunt. He had not seen many geese on February 18.

On February 19, we went out early to check things out and we found out that the migration of geese from the Mississippi Flyway was on. 80% of the snow goose population in the Mississippi Flyway are blue geese. We hunted that same bunch of geese in southern Manitoba in 1995. However, we did not see them in 1996 and only witnessed the Central Flyway snows/blues. The ratio in the Central Flyway is 70% white and 30% blue. All day the geese were flying. Some would spiral down and settle into a roost pond and the rest would head northwest towards Clay Center. There was a late snow goose season from February 1 through February 15 in this area that was now closed. Before I go any further in this chapter, let me tell you about the migration of snow geese into Nebraska.

Usually, no snows and blues stay in Nebraska during the winter. There might be a few that hang around DeSoto, near Missouri Valley, Iowa or north of Omaha. The refuge manager at DeSoto, George Gage, mentioned that 50 to 100 were seen in January. He also told about the flock of 2,500 that were inside the DeSoto refuge in late December, even though the waters on the refuge were frozen. They spent six days, 24 hours a day, on a frozen corn field. Obviously, the flock had lost their migration sense and would not fly south to find safe waters to roost on. Instead, they stayed in the field, surrounded by almost 50 coyotes. The coyotes would pick off 15 to 20 of them daily by sneaking up on them. The geese would get up and fly to the other end of the field and the coyotes would start over again. This lasted for six days before the flock finally departed for safer places.

The closest concentration of geese to southern Nebraska is Leavenworth, Kansas. These geese will depart this area and move into southern Nebraska to feed on fresh corn. If they stay at Leavenworth from November through January, there won't be much left to eat near Leavenworth. Otherwise, Nebraska will entertain all the geese from the Mississippi and the Central Flyways. If you are in southern Nebraska during the entire migrations, you will witness some spectacular scenes. In 1997, there were three fantastic observations. On February19, there were geese in the air for three solid hours. On Saturday, February 22, there were at least 30,000 geese in the air for five hours, and on February 25, it was the same scenario. That many geese in five hours would total almost a million geese that were migrating over and heading towards Clay Center and the safe zone.

The geese from the Mississippi Flyway are coming from Arkansas, Tennessee, Louisiana and eastern Texas. The Central Flyway geese come from Oklahoma, Texas, Mexico and Kansas. They arrive at these destinations around November 1 through January 1 and feed on rice, rye grass, maize, soy beans, peanuts, corn and sprouting greens from grass, cotton etc. What makes them migrate near the middle of February will never be known. Their hormones might erupt and they notice more daylight in a day and they will move on. The goose has no reasoning power and cannot think. All they have going for them is instinct, great memory, great eyesight and good hearing. They wait for the upper level south winds to blow, and they will be here one day and gone the next.

Both flyways will follow the Missouri River that divides Missouri and Kansas. When they get close to Nebraska, they will fly northwest on a heading for Clay Center, Nebraska. This small town is in the rainwater basin and is home to the U.S. Government Meat Research Center. This agency has 38,000 acres of land that hold 25,000 cattle that are used for experimental purposes. There are two large bodies of water and many small watersheds on this piece of

Rain or shine and snow or no snow, the snows and blues still have to eat. This cold scene was taken in Nebraska in March 1997.

property. No hunting is allowed on this land and the geese know this. When they migrate here in the fall, they remember this and return for an encore in the spring. Most of the geese don't stop here for long in the fall. As a result, there is a good food supply that consists of corn and winter wheat. On March 11,

A typical Nebraska corn field: large with the corn cut down short.

1993, I witnessed 3,500,000 geese in this area. Those figures were verified by several Fish and Wildlife workers that were working and counting geese in this area at that time. I went over to this area on February 27, in the morning. There were at least four million geese in the area. I heard that there were six million geese in the area on March 10, 1997. I can't verify these numbers, however, it would not surprise me. All the geese in my hunting areas had departed on March 8, 1997.

Even though the migration was spectacular, most snows and blues flew over our heads and did not touch down in our hunting area. On Sunday, February 23, there were over 100,000 snows that

We used a lot of North Wind windsocks while hunting in Nebraska in the spring. The winds really made them look alive.

were feeding in a corn field, less than a mile from where I was hunting. At the same time, there was a spectacular migration of a million or more snows and blues going on. These geese were flying north-west and heading towards Clay Center, and they flew over our heads and the heads of the 100,000 feeding geese. The migration lasted almost four hours and not one goose, out of all those that were migrating, stopped to join the 100,000 feeding geese. They knew their destination and nothing was going to detour them. Geese usually attract geese; however, this was not the case on February 23, 1997.

One thing I noticed during my 18 days of hunting in southern Nebraska was that the only time migrating geese would come down was in the afternoon hours, after they had become tired and hungry from flying. They might have been flying six to ten hours and evidently needed a break.

The migrating geese would spiral down from

10,000 feet in the air and would settle into a roost pond. Their intention was to stay as long as possible. However, most would only stay a day or two before moving on. The hunting pressure would drive them out and they would migrate northwest to the safe zones.

Back in 1996, Nebraska, Kansas, Oklahoma and Arkansas decided to have a late-season snow goose hunt for their respective states. Their was moderate success in Arkansas and Kansas. Nebraska was a "bust" because of the brutal cold. Zone 1 in Nebraska in 1997 was a bust too. Again, the weather was too cold and the waters were frozen. Hardly a snow goose was killed in Nebraska between February 1 and February 15, 1997. The purpose of the late snow goose season was to thin out the snow goose population and

It snowed twice in 18 days while in Nebraska in February of 1997.

generate income for these states. The Fish and Wildlife Services told the media about the crisis of the overpopulated snow goose and the "crash" that was about to happen because there were too many snows and blues. These kinds of stories sold a lot of licenses and generated a lot of license revenue. However, it did not solve any problems because there weren't many snow geese killed in the spring. Some of the reasons for this are:

1. The snow goose is very clever and also is very difficult to decoy.

2. The snows that you see in the spring are survivors and have been shot at over 170 times since September 1, when the snow goose season begins up on Hudson Bay in Canada.

The snow goose is clever and tough to fool. Quality decoys like this Higdon full body will help put the odds in your favor; it fooled a few wise old snows in Nebraska in 1997.

3. The caliber of hunters in Nebraska that chase the snow goose have no chance to get close to this goose because they lack the numbers and quality of snow goose decoys.

4. Nebraska has 12 counties that are closed to goose hunting due to the sandhill crane tourist business from February 15 on, so all the migrating snows and blues go into the closed counties.

With all the hype printed about snow goose over-population and the eventual crash of their population, some hunters get the idea that they have to go after the snows/blues and "murder them." This kind of attitude will present problems.

With lack of both equipment and know-how to chase the elusive snow goose, the only way a "killer" from Nebraska can get a goose for dinner is to cheat. I saw more hunting violations in the 18 days I hunted in Nebraska in 1997, than I have seen in my 33 years of goose hunting that takes in from 120 to 180 days per year. Trespassing, shooting from the road, shooting from the right-of-ways, shooting out of a truck, and shooting after hours were just a few things that disgusted me and my hunting parties from Illinois, Kansas, Iowa, North Dakota and Minnesota.

Hunting in the Nebraska areas where we were on week-ends was impossible. We often encountered six to ten different trucks, with passengers dressed in hunting outfits, out cruising around the roads and playing the game, "bust the snow goose from the road." To the pure decoy hunter that I am, this is tough to swallow. We had a local hunter belly crawl into our decoy spread. We had several run down our fence lines, trying to intercept geese that were coming into our decoy spread.

Another time, we had a guy working our decoy spread with a "cow plane." We had gone out to lunch, and some snows settled within our decoys while we were gone. A local "road hunter" spotted the geese and got his cow plane out. A cow plane consists of two pieces of 4x8 plywood hinged together, with handles inserted on each side of the cow plane; a cow is painted on the outside of the boards. Two "peek holes" are drilled in the top front of each board. The "slob hunter" with no mentality will walk slowly towards the feeding geese with the cow plane in front of him, hoping the geese think there is a cow coming at them. Most geese are not afraid of cattle. However, the snow goose is a very clever bird. I have never seen the "cow plane" work in my 17 years of hunting Nebraska.

When you have the local hunters in Nebraska hunting with the cow plane, and busting geese from the road, it makes harvesting a snow goose hard to do. In addition to this, there was an outfitter from the Dakotas that was charging $275.00 a day to hunt snow geese. Because decoying the geese was almost impossible, this outfitter and his clients were busting the geese from the waters and from their roost ponds. When you bust a goose off of a roost pond, the goose will migrate out of the area, and that is exactly what they did. This outfitter had a lot of pressure on him to produce some birds and he was forced to cheat. If he did this in Texas, they would take him in back of the barn and shoot him. Speaking of Texas, I want to tell you about something that happened while I was down there hunting for three months prior to hunting in Nebraska. I think of this story about trespassing because I hope Nebraska makes their trespassing laws as tough as those in Texas.

This 40-year-old "redneck" who lived southwest of Houston spotted some snow geese feeding near a road one morning in January of 1997. It is against the law in Texas to shoot off the road or to trespass (the fine for walking on a man's land with a gun is $1,000.00). However, this guy shot into the flock and killed two snow geese, then walked onto the land and retrieved his dead geese. The landowner observed the whole scene from his pickup as he was driving down the road. He pulled his pistol from the backseat of his truck and stopped behind the trespassing hunter's truck, then shot out the guy's two back tires. He called the sheriff and the conservation officer on his mobile phone. When the guy came back with the two geese, the landowner made him put the shotgun down and held him until the two officers arrived. They issued the hunter citations for shooting off the road and trespassing. The guy had to call his brother-in-law, who went to Wal-Mart and purchased two new tires and changed his wheels. The trespasser went to court two weeks later and paid $1,148.00 in fines. He could have filed

A nice-looking spread of Flambeau shell decoys mixed in with North Wind windsocks. They are set up in a winter wheat field.

charges against the landowner for his damaged tires; however, he thought about it and didn't. He had had enough of this landowner!

Because of the difficult hunting situations in Nebraska in the spring, successful snow goose hunting is 20 times harder than hunting in Texas, 15 times harder than northern Manitoba and 10 times harder than southern Manitoba. Under the present laws in Nebraska and the way some outfitters hunt with their clients, I would not recommend hunting in this state. The whole state should be open to hunt these white geese and there should be a law that makes it illegal to hunt within 200 yards of private waters. This would give the migrating goose a chance to sit down, catch their breath and go out to feed; that way, they might stick around for a couple of days.

Here's another story of the frustrations I encountered while hunting in southern Nebraska in 1997. I had leased the land surrounding a few ponds located north of Fairbury, Nebraska. At least 600,000 snows and blues migrated into two of these ponds one afternoon about 4 pm; I saw them spiral down from

8,000 feet in the air while I was hunting in another field across the road. So I was looking forward to a good shoot the next morning.

Legal shooting time ends at 6:25 pm. We had quit before that and started picking up our decoys. It was 7:45 pm when we were done and ready to get into our trucks to leave. We heard five shots fired from various shotguns and the 600,000 geese rose up, screaming. Someone had shot at them off of the water, 75 minutes after legal shooting time.

The next morning, we hunted my leased fields that were next to that roost pond. There were no geese left on those two ponds. They had migrated into Clay County. We waited in those two fields all day for more geese to migrate into the area and stop at these two ponds, as they had been doing. It never happened, and my six clients from Minnesota and Illinois never fired a shot.

I could tell you another 10 to 20 disgusting stories of what I witnessed. We saw some conservation officers that were trying to do their jobs. However, it is impossible to catch these "slobs" that break the laws. I know some great goose hunters that hunt Canada geese on the Platte River in the fall. I also know of many super pheasant and deer hunters that hunt ethically in Nebraska. It is too bad these slob hunters give the state of Nebraska a black eye because of the way they hunt snow geese in the spring. If they can't do it correctly, they should sell their goose guns.

Our overall hunting in Nebraska during the spring of 1997 was poor. We harvested 253 geese, which worked out to two goose per man per day. For the many hours we hunted each day, this was not good goose hunting. We harvested 42, 35 and 33 geese on good days. However, we also had a lot of two-goose, one-goose and "skunk" days. All the geese we killed were over decoys.

The weather was great while I was there. It got into the 60's on seven out of 18 days. It snowed 3" one day, rained on four days and was very windy on at least ten days. Look out for the moisture in Nebraska! Driving on their dirt roads can be risky. You could not go out onto a field without 4x4 drive.

Hunting snow geese in Nebraska doesn't require a lot of decoys. We used a lot of North Wind windsocks, shells and some full bodies. With the winds blowing all the time, the windsocks looked great. I did observe a serious goose hunter who was having a lot of success using the Outlaw snow goose silhouettes. He had 15 dozen and was doing well. The snows had never seen this decoy and he was decoying them in close. I ordered 20 dozen when I got back home.

Be sure to bring along your Hunting Classic over-the-boot waders to keep your leather Sorel boots dry. The mud will kill you in Nebraska. Warm clothing is important during this spring hunt. It might get down to zero on many days. Remember! It is still winter in Nebraska in February. It's important to have your gun-cleaning supply kit along because of all the damp soils. You might be driving onto a lot of corn fields in Nebraska. Beware! You will be getting some flat tires because those corn stalks are sharp and will cut into the sidewalls. I had three flats while hunting in Nebraska in 1997.

If you need any other information on how or where to go, or if you want to book a hunt with me, call or write:
Dennis Hunt
P.O. Box 131235
St. Paul, Minnesota 55113
Fax: 612-644-3653
Phone: 409-245-1751 (this is the Cattleman's Motel, where Dennis will be November–January)

Results Of The Trip

I had unusually high harvests of waterfowl on this long trip and I would like to tell you about them. I can attribute my success to being in the right place at the right time. As they say in real estate, location is everything. The usual hard work put into a goose hunt and having quality equipment will also help in getting great results.

Northern Manitoba

The hunt at Kaska Goose Camp was nothing less than sensational. The migration of the geese was on and getting a limit every day was as easy as putting your shoes on. You had to restrain yourself some mornings because you did not want to shoot your limit of eight geese and not have anything to do in the afternoon. At Kaska, the ATV driver will take you to the blinds at 6:15 in the morning and pick you up at 11:30 for lunch. Then they'll take you back out at a time selected by the hunters and pick you back up at 7:30 pm. If you shoot your limit in the morning, you will be done for the day. No one breaks the law at Kaska and Charlie Taylor, the manager of Kaska, makes sure of that.

At Kaska, your hunting party will hunt the blinds on the east end of the camp on day #1 and go to the blinds on the west end of the camp on day #2. This eliminates any favoritism and makes things equal. Hunting geese can be great on both the east and the west sides. You select any of the eight blinds on either end of the camps and stay all day if you desire. If the blind appears to be unproductive, you can move to another blind 200 yards away or wherever you want to go. You pay attention to the winds and to the tide because this will affect the way the geese will fly.

I had preset the decoys at each blind prior to the start of the goose hunting season. The hunters would turn the decoys into the wind daily. They might make a minor change to the spread but the spreads looked good and were very effective in decoying geese. 1996 marked the greatest harvest at Kaska in the history of the camp. I can tell you that I shot my eight-goose limit fourteen straight days at Kaska. The possession limit is 32 and most of my birds were given to the Split Lake Indian Community. I also took home a limit of 32.

If you look at a map of Hudson Bay, you will see a huge body of water that is part of the Arctic Ocean. On the southern part of this body of water is James Bay. This is where most of the snows and blues from the Central and Mississippi flyways raise their young. The birds get there in late May and depart the area in late August. Most of them will fly north, 800 miles to the Nelson River that is north of Kaska and south of Churchill. The Nelson River is a large body of water and the geese will stage there. They then fly 200 miles west and start going south and southwest to begin their fall migration. They do this because there is a food source on the coast of Hudson Bay in the form of shoots/roots and berries. The young geese that will be with them will have to put on more body fat before they can migrate, and the old goose and gander that accompany them know that. If they left James Bay and flew west without first flying north to the Nelson River, they would encounter a shortage of food and a lack of safe water to roost on. Again, the older geese know this and choose to fly north as they have done for years. Geese live by memory and instinct so they head for the Nelson River.

Some snows are raised north of Churchill and

they could be part of the Mississippi Flyway. They migrate south down the Hudson Bay to James Bay and begin their migration from there. Therefore, you have snow geese flying past Kaska that are migrating both north and south. The Canada geese, the Ross geese and the greater snow geese are also raised north and east of Churchill. We killed nine greater snow geese at Kaska that got mixed in with the other geese that were migrating south and flying past Kaska. The Canada geese you will encounter consist of small and medium-size birds.

When the geese are migrating, they seldom stay more than a day or two. They pick away at the grass or berries and get some rest. Leaving the decoys out for the season at Kaska is no problem because the geese are never around long enough to recognize them.

After the ATV driver drops you and your hunting partners off, you will get comfortable in your blind and wait. Some days, there is so much action that you can pick

Another day at the office at Kaska. A limit of Canada and snow geese brought in by the ATV and cart. Getting a cart full of geese daily was nothing unusual in northern Manitoba.

out your favorite bird to kill for a future dinner or a "wall hanger." The Ross geese are the dumbest and getting them is simple. The snows, even though they are wary, are not as difficult to decoy as they are in southern Manitoba or North Dakota. The Canada geese can be difficult to get because they stay on the coast and eat on the kelp weed that the tide brings in. If the tide is out, the Canada geese will be out within the tide and will be elusive. When the tide is in, though, the Canadas will fly over your blinds on the coastline, just like the other geese. The action out of the blinds is not predictable. The wind dictates when the geese will migrate. When the wind is blowing from the south, you will have a heavy migration of snows from the direction of James Bay. When the winds are from the west and north, the Ross and Canada geese will be flying down the coast-line from the north. There could be some snows that will accompany those birds.

You will see some ducks in the area, but they will be on the Kaskattama River and near the Kaska Goose Camp. There will be pintails, black ducks, teal and mallards to shoot at. Most ducks aren't raised this far north and the duck hunting is only fair compared to southern Manitoba which is the duck factory of the world. Kaska hunters that pursued the ducks up the river or back in the pools of water would get their share. I am a goose hunter. I wasn't interested in chasing any ducks up at the Kaska Goose Camp.

When I left Kaska and headed for Dymond Hunting Lodge, 180 miles north of Kaska, I was walking in the clouds. I had a super time and got in some great shooting. I was feeling great and my reflexes were good. That adds up to some good shooting. I was shooting over 75% up at Kaska, using my Winchester model 50 automatic. It is an old and reliable gun. I have killed over 7,000 geese with that gun, all over decoys. I use an Ithaca Mag 10 for goose hunting also. However, the Mag 10 is 4.5 pounds heavier than the Winchester, and I don't use it early in the season because I don't swing it fast enough and I end up behind the birds. I didn't use the Mag 10 until I got into southern Manitoba.

I didn't know what to expect when I got to Dymond Hunting Lodge. I had heard from some friends that had been to Dymond September 1 thru September 4 and they had great shooting. The Ross geese migrate through early and I was hoping that I wasn't too late for them. After talking to Stewart Webber, the camp manager at Dymond, I was assured that I would get some good shooting. The weather was warm and the birds were migrating south, knowing that the clock was ticking on the goose hunting season in northern Manitoba.

My first day out, I hunted with an employee at Dymond. His name is Tommy Brightnose and he is a native from the Split Lake Indian reservation which is 180 southwest of Churchill. Brightnose is 35 years old, and is an accomplished hunter and a good shot. We went to a blind out on the coast and set up a spread of 36 North Wind windsocks. We had our limit of 16 geese—12 snows and 4 Ross—by 10:30 a.m. We had three groups come in and shot six, six, and four out of the groups. Only a few prisoners escaped. Brightnose was running out of shells and was shooting Federal #6 and #7½ lead shells. Lead shot was legal in Manitoba in 1996; that was going to be the last year before hunters had to switch over to steel shot in 1997, unless there would be a year reprieve as the locals were hoping would happen. Anyway, Brightnose was hitting the geese, but he could not kill them with his light load. He was running all over the tundra chasing crippled geese. He got them all and I am thankful for that. I got to hunt with Tommy Brightnose two more times before I left and we limited out both times.

The author, dressed in his Brigade Quartermaster camouflage with his Rice Lake Products hat on, shows off some Canada geese he harvested. Note the wide-open tundra terrain, the Higdon full body decoys in the background and Hudson Bay. It gets cold up there in the winter time!

The second day I hunted I was paired with four hunters from Rockford, Illinois. They were average shots and great guys. We decided to hunt "Hamburger Hill" because it was within walking distance of the lodge and two of the hunters didn't want to stay in the blinds for more than three hours at a time. They could hunt at Hamburger Hill and walk the short distance back to the lodge and get their "cat nap," which they wanted to do. That was fine with me because I wanted to kill geese.

We got out to our blinds along side of Hamburger Hill. The blinds were within small bushes and there were lounge chairs and a sofa in the blind. The lodge had gotten new furniture a few years ago and decided to put the old furniture to good use. Imagine, sitting in a lounge chair or a sofa and killing geese as they flew over the decoys 30 yards away. Only in northern Manitoba!

It was 7:15 a.m. when the first geese appeared as they were flying down the coast and going south. As they got within two miles of us, they decided to cut the corner and fly over Hamburger Hill. There were snows in the small family group and they came at us 40 yards high. The five of us opened up and the whole family got wiped out. There would be no migration for this family in 1996. This happened twice more that morning, and we went to lunch with 32 geese on the ground. After lunch, I was joined by only one of the group for the afternoon shoot. The geese were still flying over us and we shot the other eight geese to fill our limit. We did get seven Ross geese out of the 40 but we did not kill any Canada geese that day.

Helen Webber, a great cook, fixed our hunting group, and several others, a dinner of goose pot pie. It was great and was the first time I ever had the opportunity to eat geese that way. Thank you, Helen!

The shooting at Dymond continued great and we got into the medium-size Canada geese the next five days. They came at us, flock after flock, and the hunting was a "no brainer." The limit on Canada geese was five; we would have that in the morning and then have to switch over to shooting snows in the afternoon. I kept hunting with the guys from Rockford and they had the best shooting of their life. We were on Hamburger Hill some days, and down on the coast or out on the flats on other days. It didn't matter, the geese kept coming and coming. We were all shooting Federal #2 lead and when we hit a goose, the goose was dead. Part of the fun of hunting in Manitoba is using lead shot. I will be a sorry goose hunter when they eliminate lead in Manitoba. It has been an enjoyable 21 years of shooting lead in that province.

I left Dymond Hunting Lodge and headed for southern Manitoba. I would be hunting there for 28 days. I knew I would end up disappointed because the results could not be any better than what I had just experienced at Kaska and Dymond Hunting Camps. I had never hunted northern Manitoba before, only southern Manitoba. I was going to my southern Manitoba stomping grounds and already, I had killed over 200 geese. What do you do for an encore?

Southern Manitoba

I was glad to get down to southern Manitoba. I had hunted this area for over 20 years and you get what you work for. No limits are obtained unless you use the basic steps: *field selection, quality decoys* with at least 75% movement within the spread, and *excellent concealment.*

There were nearly 75,000 geese in my hunting area when I arrived there two days before the season started. I know the patterns of the geese in this area because I see the same congregations of them each year. Geese will fly the same routes each year en route to their final destination. The exception would be if strong winds blow them off course. This has never happened to these geese because they migrate into the area in the middle of September, and there are never strong winds at that time because the weather hasn't changed yet. I located the areas where the geese were staying, in six ponds on private land. There is a bird sanctuary in the area, but the

Pat Lavalle, Jeff Jones and Scott McLaughlin admire this nice harvest of ducks and geese taken while hunting with Dennis Hunt in southern Manitoba.

snows haven't used it in recent years because the water is too deep. You will find some Canadas in there from time to time, however. After finding the roost ponds, I would locate the spots where the geese were feeding and where they had already fed. I knew they would be into barley fields because that is their grain of choice in southern Manitoba at this time of the season. Later, after the corn fields were harvested, the geese would go into corn fields.

I had a good game plan for harvesting some geese for my friends and me. As I expected, the geese were eating barley and using the same barley fields in the same areas as they usually do. My next job was to check out the ducks and get some ponds where we could shoot our limit of six per day. My God! I haven't seen this many ducks since the 1950's.

There are over 200 bodies of water in my hunting area and every pond was dotted with ducks. This was going to be fun! Goose hunting ends at 12 noon on the first 11 days of the season, so in the afternoon, you hunt ducks, sharptail grouse or Hungarian partridge, or take a nap.

My friends in my hunting party arrived on Sunday and they went out to check out the geese. You can't shoot a gun in Manitoba on Sunday in our area, so my friends took their cameras instead of their scatterguns. They came back all excited and we were looking forward to the opening of the waterfowl season in southern Manitoba.

While hunting snow geese in southern Manitoba, North Dakota, Nebraska or Kansas, the rule of thumb is; if you select the proper field, set out a quality decoy spread, and stay concealed, you should get between five and 25 geese per day for four hunters. This should be easy to do.

The first week of the season, we killed between 12 and 25 for four gunners on five different occasions. But on Wednesday of the first week, we only shot one goose. The reason? It snowed four inches the day before and the birds "freaked out" and never came out to feed until 11 a.m., with less than 50 flying over our decoys. The snow melted within 24 hours and things got back to normal.

The duck hunting was super, with thousands of mallards buzzing our decoys in the barley fields. We shot as few as seven and as many as 16 each of the six days of the hunting season. The variety of ducks in Manitoba includes canvasbacks, redheads, pintails, teal, gadwall, bluebills, widgeon and more mallards. We had over 20,000 mallards buzzing our decoys in our barley fields on many occasions. This was quite a spectacular sight.

The second week in southern Manitoba was better than the first. Our low goose hunt was 17 and our high was 37. That was hunting with three other gunners. Some of the time, I was shooting video with my Canon Hi-8 and working on some future goose hunting videos. After the first two weeks, my different hunting parties averaged 12 geese per man that they took home, as well as their limit of 12 ducks. Some guys would shoot a limit of six ducks and give them away to stay within the possession limit of 12. This way they could hunt another day. My friends who hunted with me would stay only three days. Some of them had the best shooting of their lives, taking into consideration the terrific duck shooting they had.

The third week was even more productive than the second week. The reason? You can hunt geese all day, starting with the second Saturday of the hunting season. We tried to keep the pressure off the geese by not hunting the same flocks two days in a row. This lets them rest and stay at ease without turning wild and/or migrating out of the area. We averaged five geese per man, per day, and everyone got

These four hunters from Minnesota took these mallards, snows and blues while hunting with Dennis Hunt in southern Manitoba in 1996. The hunter with the white mustache, Dennis Ozbun, and the man to his left, Norm Davies, are high profile hunters who have hunted around the world.

their limit of six ducks. On Thursday, October 17, we witnessed a migration of greenheads that lasted almost two hours. The drake mallard will leave the hen mallard in early summer and migrate north to be with the boys, leaving the hen to raise the young by herself. The drake mallards were coming from north of Brandon and were flying over us in spectacular formations. We did catch up to them the fourth week of the season as we moved our location and were closer to the North Dakota border.

The fourth week of the season found us fighting four inches of snow and some strong winds. The geese were starting to leave and we were down to 10,000 total in our area. There were still over 100,000 mallards in our area. Four of us finished out the season in southern Manitoba and we averaged five geese and six mallards per man, per day. There were a few days where we could have shot 100 mallards each, if the limits were that high! It reminded me of the late 1950's, when ducks would blacken the sky as they flew over Minnesota en route south.

1996 was the most spectacular shooting I have encountered in Manitoba in 20 years and I want to thank God for bringing the ducks back. I hope it is as good in 1997 as it was in 1996. The goose hunting was about average, with the peak migration coming on October 2, instead of October 8. Why? No one will ever know because it is all unpredictable. The sad note is the elimination of lead shot. All of my friends shot Federal #2 lead for geese, Federal #4 for ducks and Federal #6 lead for sharptails. By the way, we killed 47 sharptails in Manitoba in 1996. That was an extra bonus.

Southern Texas

The overall rating I'd give the 90-day goose hunt in

Dennis Hunt and friends with a nice harvest of specks, blues, snows and small Canadas. The medium and large-sized Canada goose is rare in south Texas. They don't migrate that far south.

Texas in 1996/97 would be very good. The 500 goose hunters that were clients of Third Coast Outfitters harvested slightly over 5,900 birds. That was an average of over six birds per man, per day. From what I observed, that was very good. I think the numbers could have been even better, but I've observed that some clients/hunters couldn't hit the broad side of a barn from ten yards away.

As I mentioned earlier in this book, Texas goose hunting is hard physically. However, it's easy to harvest geese. Here are some of the reasons:

1. There are over 3,500,000 geese in the vicinity of Bay City, Texas at this time of year.

2. There is a limited amount of agricultural land to provide food for the geese.

3. The outfitters have all the prime spots leased, and they only chase and bother specified flocks of

John Niemann (far left) from Parma, Michigan, alongside Chuck Berry from Texas Hunting Products, bragging about the geese their group killed near Markham, Texas.

geese twice per week. The geese are semi-tame.

4. The whitefront geese in this area are very naive and stupid. They respond to calls and decoy easily. An average goose hunter can decoy and shoot his limit of one whitefront goose every day of the season. If the Fish and Wildlife Service ever raised the limits on whitefront geese to four per day, the whitefront goose would be extinct in two years.

5. The small Canada goose in the area are no smarter than the whitefront geese.

The geese arrive as early as October 15, and the goose season begins in south Texas the first weekend of November. Some years, most of the snows/blues don't arrive in large numbers until November 15. In 1995 and 1996, a front went through North Dakota in late October and blew all the snows straight to Texas. Most of them arrived on Halloween. The fields were full of snow geese when the season opened in those two years.

Because of the light hunting pressure and the security of the agricultural lands, the geese are vulnerable in south Texas. There are some immature snows and blues that haven't been shot at before arriving in Texas. Prior to coming to Texas, these geese stayed and staged in southern Manitoba. Hunting pressure is light in southern Manitoba compared to North Dakota, and the geese don't fly into North Dakota as they did in the past. They put on a large amount of body fat in southern Manitoba and wait for the northwest winds to blow in late October to get a free ride to Texas.

We had no trouble decoying these immature snows in Texas, and at least 60% of the harvest were young birds. The decoys used in Texas were Texas rags and North Wind windsocks. I always used a spread of Outlaw Canada silhouettes to complement the spread and entice the whitefronts and small Canadas to get closer. The silhouettes are successful because the black geese in Texas are not used to seeing silhouettes, and it might take three or four years before the geese wise up to the Outlaw silhouette. Since I left Texas, I ordered 20 dozen additional Outlaw silhouettes in the snow goose pattern. They are super, and I look forward to using them in 1997/98.

Geese live by memory. and they remember decoys and decoy spreads. Years ago, you could decoy the snow geese with paper napkins, white paper plates, plain white rags, and rubber tires. But the geese got wise to these old tricks, and to stay ahead of them you have to change your decoy spreads in both numbers and cosmetics. The goose hunter that uses many types of movement decoys will trick more snows into getting close enough for a shot. Another thing I think the geese have caught on to is hunters dressed in white outfits, laying within the decoy spreads. Hunters have been doing this for over 15 years, and I am convinced that many wise old birds avoid the large "blobs of white" laying within a decoy spread and shooting at them.

If a serious decoy hunter like myself could drive out onto the field and unload his full bodies and complement them with North Wind windsocks and Outlaw silhouettes, the rate of harvest could be double. The snows and specks don't see many full body decoys in south Texas, so it would fool them. The Texas rag is used more than the North Wind windsock because it costs less, but it only lasts for two years or less. However, the Texas rag can still be effective if it is properly installed on a wooden dowel and maintained properly. The old snows are

Four hunters from Michigan with specks, snows, Canadas and blues. This nice harvest is just an average morning's hunt for Third Coast Outfitters.

These happy hunters from Ohio and Washington with a nice harvest near Bay City, Texas. Third Coast has hosted goose hunters from over 45 states and England.

accustomed to seeing Texas rags all day, and still decoy into some of them.

The weather was another factor that aided our harvest success. There were a lot of foggy days in south Texas, and a foggy day is the answer to a goose hunter's prayers. The geese will fly low and they can't see very well in the foggy conditions. They will spot the decoys through the fog, and will be vulnerable before they figure out that the decoys are not real geese. On January 28 in a thick fog, two of our hunting parties shot 101 geese with ten gunners and two guides. It doesn't get much better than that!

The wind also aids a goose hunter, and it helped us on many occasions in south Texas. The old statement "more wind, more birds" was certainly true in south Texas. The wind blew over 20mph on 20 out of 90 days. There might not be much wind at 7 a.m., but by 10 a.m. the winds can come on strong and throw the geese off their patterns. We had some great results while hunting between 10 a.m. and 12 noon in south Texas.

One of the reasons Third Coast Outfitters harvest a lot of geese is that the hunting pressure is very light in the Bay City area. A few hunting clubs lease a few thousand acres, and one other outfitter also competes for the birds. However, compared to the Eagle Lake, Texas area, it gets pretty lonely around the Bay City area. Third Coast Outfitters takes out only six hunting parties with gunners, and this works out great. You have to keep it small if you're going to be successful in obtaining geese for your clients. If there are 200,000 snows in a particular area,

Don't believe this sign. There are more geese in southern Texas. There is too much hunting pressure in the Eagle Lake area.

they might be in just four fields. I know of another outfitter in south Texas who signed on 216 goose hunters on a particular Saturday morning in January. 45 guides took the hunters out, and only five of the parties harvested enough geese to brag about. Many of the guides brought their parties back with a duck, or maybe one or two geese. How do you look these paid clients in the eye? I am a guide and outfitter and I try to use the KISS system (Keep It Small, Stupid).

Comparing south Texas to the other areas I hunted, I would say that Texas goose hunting is:
- 20 times easier than southern Nebraska in spring
- 12 times easier than southern Nebraska in fall
- 10 times easier than North Dakota in the fall
- 4 times easier than southern Manitoba in the fall
- 2 times easier than northern Manitoba in the fall

I have hunted these areas extensively, with the exception of northern Manitoba, and I can attest to these figures. I would recommend south Texas goose hunting to all my readers. It is physically harder because you must walk onto the fields rather than drive. The muddy, wet conditions are more difficult than the dusty barley fields in southern Manitoba or the flat corn fields in Nebraska in the fall. However, the huge flocks of snows, blues, specks and small Canada geese that come at you will make you forget the wet conditions. In addition, you might see

Four hunters from north Texas with four straps full of geese. Another typical day at the office with Third Coast Outfitters!

10,000 to 20,000 pintail ducks swarming your decoys on many a day in south Texas. If you decide to try south Texas goose hunting, you cannot do it by yourself because all of the lands are leased and spoken for. Hire out with a small outfitter that takes out no more than six hunting parties per day. I would recommend Third Coast Outfitters. Call or write Bobby Hale at the numbers on page 61. I plan to be either guiding, hunting, or loafing at this camp the rest of my winters. I hope to see you there some hunting season!

Nebraska

The late season snow goose hunt was a big disappointment. We killed 253 geese, which averaged two per man, per day. All of them were taken over decoys. We had a 42-goose and a 35-goose shoot on two consecutive days with two hunting parties and eight gunners. We also had some two-, three- and four-goose days with one hunting party and four gunners.

This was my first year of the late season snow goose hunt in Nebraska, and I didn't know how good or bad it would be. 1996 was the first year of the hunt in Nebraska and it was a bust because of the cold weather. Some geese migrated into Nebraska the week of February 20, and the hunting was fair for eight days—until a cold front came through and the temperature went down to 10 below zero. The waters froze up and the geese migrated south to Kansas, Missouri and Arkansas. Flying 400 to 600 miles to safety means nothing to a snow goose.

There was a fabricated and exaggerated story that had appeared earlier in a magazine that features waterfowl, and there were a lot of goose hunters that read that story and were sure they would murder the snow geese. A lot of them came to southern Nebraska from a long distance in 1997 and I sure saw a lot of disappointment.

Looking back on the 1997 season in Nebraska, I can understand what happened and why. My years of hunting snow geese and the hours I have put in watching them makes it easy to understand the situation. Geese live by memory and they have been stopping in southern Nebraska for many years. During their fall migration, most of the snows and blues from the Central and Mississippi flyways will stop at DeSoto National Wildlife Refuge. There will be between 600,000 to 800,000 that will stop there for as long as two weeks. They clean the food supply out, and come spring they remember this. Why would they want to go back there in the spring when there is no food to eat? They find another destination in the spring, and that is in the Rainwater Basin of Nebraska near the Clay Center area. Almost all the geese from the Central and Mississippi flyways end up there in the spring. There were almost 6 million geese in this area on March 8, 1997 and you could not hunt these geese because this was one of the 12 counties in Nebraska that were closed to hunting. The reason that these 12 counties are closed is because of the huge tourism business near Kearney, Nebraska that attracts bird watchers who observe the sandhill cranes. Dollars and cents dictate how rules and laws are made in the legislatures, and the snow goose hunter got shafted while the buses and cars of bird watchers got a chance to take some pictures and spend $10,000,000.00 annually.

Geese can see a long way when they are flying 6,000 to 10,000 feet. They fly up the Missouri River and start heading northwest, as soon as they hit the corners of Kansas, Missouri and Nebraska. They can see the huge flocks of white in the distance in the Rainwater Basin and they head for that big glob of white. Geese attract geese and most of these geese would fly over our heads and go into the counties that were closed to snow goose hunting. The geese that did stop in our areas were geese that were tired, thirsty and hungry. We would see them funnel down from 10,000 feet, looking for a safe roost pond. The only problem was, there were no safe roost ponds. The geese would be allowed to stay in a pond until no later than the next morning, when someone would bust them off the water. The snows and blues, as well as specks and small Canada geese, would get off the water screaming and migrate northwest into the safe counties. That would put a void into the chance of decoying any of these geese. That is why we had some poor hunting days. Trespassing doesn't mean anything to a lot of young hunters that were out there cruising the roads looking for a free meal of snow goose. They would belly crawl up to the edge of these roost ponds and shoot at the resting snows. Most of the shots were over 100 yards away and these hunters never got anything. However, they left a lot of wounded snow geese on these roost ponds that no one could retrieve without a dog, and these hunters did not have an animal with them. The other outfitter in our hunting area was charging $275.00 per day to kill snow geese and this put him under extreme pressure to produce. Some of the properties that he had arranged for had roost ponds on them. The snows that landed on these ponds never had a chance to catch their breath. You don't have to be a "robot scientist" or a mathematician to figure out why we had poor snow goose hunting in Nebraska in 1997.

I don't want this to sound like "sour grapes"

because we didn't drastically reduce the population of the snow goose. However, it was very tough. All the geese that flew into the state of Nebraska were survivors. They had been shot at daily since September 1 and that was over 170 days. They had heard every game and goose call, as well as a lot of duck calls. They witnessed every style of decoy and nothing will fool some of these geese. The average age of a snow goose is over 10 years and they have forgotten more about decoys and decoy spreads than you will ever know. They hear the same idiots blowing on their goose calls and they won't be lured closer by these calls. Only about 2% of all goose hunters who own calls are qualified to blow on those goose calls. Another statistic that will open your eyes is this: 85% of the time, the goose that leaves the roost pond and is flying out to feed, knows where he is going and nothing will change that goose's mind. Some of these geese encountered this situation in early September. Some of these geese were only three months old and did not know any better. Some of the older geese had not heard the roar of a shotgun for several months and had forgotten what it sounds like. Anyway, the goose flew towards a decoy spread after hearing a hunter tooting away on a goose call. The roar of the shotgun, and getting a couple of tail feathers knocked off of his rear end, scared the hell out of that goose. That particular goose will never go near a decoy spread again. He will avoid all sounds that emanate from a goose call, and he will hate loud noises that come from a shotgun. He lives by memory and instinct and this scenario has taught him, or her, a good lesson. The only thing that will ever kill this goose is old age, disease, someone shooting that goose illegally, or someone shooting that goose from a firing line.

Most of the geese we encountered were similar to what I have just told you. There were thousands of small Canadas and specks flying over our heads very low, and some would land into our decoys. Some days, we could have killed over 100 of these black geese. However, the season was closed on them. A lot of them would fly with the snow geese. The snows would be flying in the rear and would be 50 yards higher. The specks or small Canadas would come towards our decoys and some would identify the spread and squawk out the danger call. Others would see one of my hunters and squawk out the same warning. The snow geese and blue geese that were trailing this flock of black geese would make a 180 degree turn and they would be gone. That is not right! However, it is correct. These geese wanted to go to heaven, but they did not want to die. It is extremely difficult killing a snow goose in Nebraska in the spring.

The problem with the local goose hunters in Nebraska can be explained easily. They do not have the equipment to attract a goose. The migration of

Our typical decoy spread in Nebraska, with almost 300 North Wind windsocks. Many Nebraska goose hunters don't have the necessary decoys to attract geese, so they cheat.

snow geese in the fall is very inconsistent. Some stop near the Clay Center area, but you can't bet the farm on this. Some years, like 1996 and 1995, most of the snows blew over the state and flew straight to Texas. They got a free ride on a northwest wind and they took advantage of this wind. Many snows stop at DeSoto near Blair, Nebraska. However, most of them feed on the Iowa side of the river, which makes it difficult for the Nebraska goose hunter who doesn't have an Iowa waterfowl license. As a result of the inconsistent migration of snow geese through Nebraska in the fall of the year, the goose hunters have spend their money and their time hunting Canada geese on the Platte River. The spring late season snow goose hunt brings out the amateurs, and they break the law because of a lack of equipment. How do you decoy a super-smart snow goose in March that has been shot at for over 185 days in a row if you don't have any equipment? The answer is, you have to cheat. And cheating means shooting out of a truck, shooting off of roads, shooting off of right-of-ways, trespassing and shooting after hours. That is what I witnessed in 1997 in Nebraska during the late season snow goose hunting season. I saw more violations in 18 days of hunting than I have seen in 33 total years of hunting. Is it any wonder we didn't limit out on snow geese? We were lucky to have gotten two geese per man, per day.

I would not recommend trying this spring hunt in Nebraska unless the following changes are made:

1. No hunting within 300 yards on private waters more than one acre in size.

2. Open the 12 counties that are closed and eliminate the geese flying into a "safe zone."

3. Enforce the laws and eliminate some of the laws being broken.

If you decide to try it on your own, I would give you the following advice.

A 4x4 vehicle is absolutely necessary, and your tires must be in good shape. I had four flats and wore out a set of hubs in 18 days. Bring along a tow chain if you have one. Also bring along a roll of quarters for the do-it-yourself car washes. You will have to wash your truck twice a day so you can see out of the windows.

Bring a good selection of high-quality decoys. I recommend 300 North Wind windsocks, two Outlaw or Killer Kites, lots of camouflage to match the corn fields, and a 5-foot Sportsmax sled to haul your decoys out into the muddy fields.

Standard clothing includes the Brigade Quartermaster lined pants and jacket, as well as long johns. Two pair of Sorel rubber boots and one pair of Sorel leather boots are needed in the often muddy fields; a pair of Hunter's Classic over-the-boot waders will help keep your boots dry. You'll need several pairs of gloves to keep your hands warm and dry also.

Make sure your shotguns are in good working condition; I recommend two good 10- or 12-gauge shotguns for Nebraska. You'll need a supply of Federal BBB or T shot shells, and of course, your gun cleaning kit. And bring along your cellular phone; you will need it to call TIP to report hunting violations.

Comparing The Areas

After looking back on the long trip, I realize how
fortunate I was to make the trip and I want to thank
God for giving me the opportunity to do it.

There was so much to see and learn and the
education I received will never be forgotten. I learned
so much more about the geese and all of this will
enable me to become a better goose hunter. The fine
people I met and the opportunity to get involved with
some great goose hunters will always stay with me. I
will try to pass some of this information on to you in
this chapter. I will compare the four areas and give
you my opinions. This will give you insight into what
I went through.

When you go on a goose hunting trip, the
objectives are:
1. Go to a place where you will get a chance to hunt.
2. Get opportunities to shoot your shotgun.
3. Harvest a few birds.
4. Enjoy the companionship of your hunting
   friends, and meet new people.
5. Get some exercise.
6. Bring back some good memories.

OPPORTUNITIES TO HUNT
In comparing the four areas, the goose hunter that
wants to do it himself will be restricted to southern
Manitoba and Nebraska. In Northern Manitoba,
there are only two goose hunting camps and you
have to book a hunt with one of them, if you are
going to go. Both camps are leased by the province
of Manitoba and are regarded as wildlife refuges with
privileges to hunt waterfowl and ptarmigan only on
the hunting camp sites. Both of the camps are on
the Hudson Bay and most areas of Hudson Bay are
unaccessible. You cannot get close because there are

no roads. There is a road or train going to Churchill; however, where are you going to hunt? Your only options are the two goose camps, and you can get to either of them on an airplane. Hunting is great at both camps, and I would recommend either of them. This is a place every goose hunter should visit before he dies unless there is a better place in heaven.

Texas goose hunting is the same scenario as that of Northern Manitoba. You have to contact an outfitter and go with him. All the private land in goose hunting country is leased. Most goose hunters that like to do it themselves do not realize the services a good outfitter can provide. Here are some of them:

- Leases productive agricultural fields that will attract geese. This could cost up to $10.00 per acre and this is a risky business.
- Hires qualified hunters to act as guide to assist you on a safe hunt.
- Invests in quality decoys and hunting equipment to make the hunts productive.

John Niemann, Dennis Hunt and Bobby Hale with another great shoot. Third Coast Outfitters takes care to lease agricultural lands that will produce geese. They also use quality decoy spreads.

- Spends countless hours scouting the geese and locating the fields where they will be tomorrow to make your hunt successful.
- Insures the hunters.
- Advertises his business to inform you.

This all costs lots of money and is an investment that provides the outfitter and his employees a chance to make a living. The job is difficult and is a gamble. For the amount paid an outfitter or a guide versus the hours he spends involved in making your hunt successful, his pay is less than $10.00 per hour. How many professional men would work for that wage?

These happy hunters from California and Pennsylvania admire the 19 ducks and geese they harvested while laying in a muddy Texas field. Note the standing water in the ditch and field. It had rained three inches in two days and it was tough walking and hunting.

There might be as many as 100 waterfowl outfitters in south Texas that you could employ. Some of them might be beginners/pretenders who take out only two hunters per outing. Some of the larger operations will have eight to 40 guides taking out 30 to 150 hunters per day. Some are good and put out a good effort, and some are wasting your time and money. I will talk about booking a hunt later in the book.

There are lots of rules to follow when you hunt in Texas. This sign explains the procedures you must follow at San Bernard Refuge. The blind hunting at this refuge can be good.

San Bernard Refuge is 25 miles southeast of Third Coast Outfitters. Lots of geese hold on this refuge.

South Texas provides some great goose hunting. Before coming to Texas to hunt geese for 90 days, I suspected that the hunting results would be unproductive. I had tried Texas hunting in the Pan Handle of Texas in the late 1970's and didn't get much. I tried it in 1995 near Eagle Lake and had some success but wasn't elated. I had talked to and seen a lot of unhappy goose hunters that were holding a goose or two after three days of hunting and had a sad look on their faces. I talked to four hunters from Alabama that had gotten just seven shots in three days for four hunters, and no geese. They were not happy hunters. However, working for Third Coast Outfitters and Bobby Hale, I left Texas happy and will always brag about "how great the goose hunting is in south Texas." I would recommend hunting in south Texas. But beware! Select the correct outfitter that will take you near the Bay City area. There are usually three million geese and 100,000 ducks in that area and most of them are not very smart. The hunting pressure is light in that area compared to the Eagle Lake area where there is a hunting group in every agricultural field.

The Canadian flag flies over Kaska and Dymond Hunting Camps. This was taken at the lodge at Kaska. The fir trees are 20 feet high, the tallest in the area. As you get closer to Hudson Bay, the tundra trees become shorter and only bushes grow on the coast. The north side of all trees are shredded of their leaves because of the strong north wind that blows on the tundra.

Southern Manitoba provides some great goose hunting as well as great duck hunting. There are only a few outfitters from Manitoba that are available for hire and I could not recommend any of them because I don't know much about them. The season is a short one and you must be there when the season opens for non-Canadians, usually on September 30. It could only last two weeks because the migration and the weather can be unpredictable.

The agricultural lands in Manitoba begin 200 miles north of Winnipeg with areas of forests. The geese will stop between Lakes Winnipeg and Manitoba and get into the grain in that area. This will be their first meals of grain after leaving the tundra, and they will stick around in the Riverton area for a week or two before migrating to the south and southwest. They will fly down to the North Dakota borders and stage there when the weather turns nasty. They used to stage in North Dakota until the hunting pressure in that state became so intense that it forced them to stay north of the border.

Southern Manitoba is a great place to hunt geese. The total cost for a Manitoba waterfowl license and necessary stamps is usually $99.00 American money. It is necessary to obtain permission to hunt on private land in the province of Manitoba so you had better have some friends, or get up there early and line up some places to go goose hunting. There are few motels, which makes reservations important.

The state of Nebraska provides you with a great opportunity to hunt geese. I have hunted in that state for over 15 years and have had a lot of success. Most of the hunting was done in the fall of the year and it was unpredictable: either feast or famine. In 1996, Nebraska and a few other southern states initiated a late season snow goose hunt. It was a bust because of the cold weather. There were some birds killed the last few days of the season, March 7 to 10. I have a guide service established there and that is why I was there. The opportunities are great because most of the geese in the Central Flyway and some from the Mississippi Flyway will fly into this state and stop to feed on corn that remains in the fields. Geese love corn and they know where to stop to get it. They need body fat to get to the tundra and they stay in Nebraska as long as 30 days before they move northward. In 1993, I was there on March 11 and witnessed almost 3.5 million geese. There were lots of Canada and whitefronts amongst those geese, which are protected in the spring in Nebraska. The waterfowl stamp and general hunting license is only $65.00 for a non-resident. The people are great, the restaurants serve great food and the goose hunting can be good in Nebraska. I would recommend that state! The snow goose seasons in 1996/97 were October 5 through December 13, and February 1 through February 16 in zone one. In zone two, the season ran from October 5 through December 13, and February 2 through March 10. The Canada goose season ended on January 12.

OPPORTUNITIES TO SHOOT YOUR GUN

This is another reason to go goose hunting and I sure got plenty of opportunities to pull the trigger on this long trip. I started out with 15 cases of new Federal Shotgun shells in both lead and steel for 10- and 12-gauge. You can still use lead in Manitoba and I used up five cases of it. I took the remaining ten cases to Texas and Nebraska and ended up purchasing six more boxes before I finished up my goose hunting season. I can honestly state, "I have never had a Federal shotgun shell malfunction in my 32 years of hunting!" I usually shoot eight to ten cases per year and Federal should be proud of this record.

The opportunities to shoot my gun were the best in northern Manitoba. I could have done more shooting in Texas if I had not elected to shoot my camcorder instead and get some footage for future goose hunting videos. However, I have no complaints about not being able to shoot my scattergun in Texas. Southern Manitoba had a few days where the snowfall spooked the geese and they didn't come out, and Nebraska was inconsistent, especially when weather affected the hunt.

Dennis Hunt admires a cart load of snows that were shot on opening day at Kaska Goose Camp. The season begins in September in northern Manitoba and the only two camps in Manitoba are open until only September 26; they close sooner if the weather turns nasty. The weather was in the 70s the whole month of September 1996 when this picture was taken.

I have no complaints about the times I shot my shotgun in almost seven months of goose hunting. I must have set some record for the amount of times I cleaned my guns during those months because of dust, dirt, mud, snow, water etc.

HARVESTING A FEW BIRDS

In this section, I will talk briefly about the numbers of geese we got and also about the ease or difficulty of harvesting geese in the four areas.

Northern Manitoba

What more can I say when I obtained my limit every day I hunted in northern Manitoba? The harvests were plentiful, and the hunting was easy. As Stewart Webber, the camp manager at Dymond Hunting Lodge at Churchill, Manitoba says, "It is a no-brainer." Not every year is like that at both of the northern Manitoba camps. However, I was in the right place at the right time, and I would rather be lucky than good. There are years where the shooting can be less than good because of the migration etc. Hunting would not be any fun if you limited out every time. You have to take the bad with the good.

Southern Manitoba

This was another good shoot in 1996. The duck hunting was the best I have ever been involved in. I hope I am wrong, but it could not be any better than it was. The goose hunting was also good with all the hunters averaging over four geese per man per day. We killed 47 sharptails in only six days of hunting them. How can you complain about that?

How would I rate Manitoba goose hunting? Northern Manitoba is better than southern Manitoba Both parts of Manitoba are easier than Nebraska. Texas is consistently better than both parts of Manitoba.

Southern Texas

What can you say when you are in a hunting camp working for an outfitter for 90 days and the hunters average over six birds per man per *All in a day's work at Third Coast!*

Bobby Hale, owner of Third Coast Outfitters and Dennis Hunt with a nice harvest of snows, blues, specks and Canadas.

day for those 90 days? I have to give credit to Bobby Hale for obtaining the necessary and productive agricultural fields where the geese came in to our decoys so the client/hunters could harvest them. Credit is also given to the fact there are over three million geese within the Bay City, Texas area. The high profile guides that took the hunters to the right spots should be given some recognition also. And how about the great hunters that hired out Third Coast Outfitters? Guys like: Mike Kennedy from Mendota Heights, Minnesota; Peter Frobouck, Phil Bollman and Jeff Case from Pittsburgh, Pennsylvania; and Andy Fanner from Valley Center, Kansas. These are just a few. Greg Schrantz and Scott Storm from Minnesota, Mike Schrantz from Davenport, Iowa and Tom Dennis from Norvon, Pennsylvania were some other good hunters I met.

When you are working along side professional guides like Ben Gregory and Bobby Hale, it is no wonder you harvest a lot of birds. Ben Gregory is the

Ben Gregory, the high profile waterfowl guide from Third Coast Outfitters in Bay City, Texas. Ben is with Honey.

best guide I've ever encountered, with Bobby Hale being the best shot and white-front goose caller. Kurt Graff was the highest profile guide I had met until I met Ben Gregory. Both of these men are great in handling hunters as well as harvesting birds. If you look into Ben Gregory's eyes, you will see the word "killer." He is a very intense and hard working guide who takes his job seriously.

Texas is the best area I have ever hunted geese and was able to kill them so easily with such consistently. In comparison, I would rank Texas twice as easy as northern Manitoba; four times as easy as southern Manitoba; ten times easier than Nebraska in the fall of the year; and 20 times easier than Nebraska in the spring of the year.

Try south Texas goose hunting. You will like it!

Nebraska

As I've said previously, the harvest in Nebraska was tough during the spring hunt. We did get birds, but our harvest was down because our hunting opportunities were often ruined by the inconsiderate or ignorant hunters we encountered. Hunting can be tough if the fields are muddy, and cold weather can be hard to take without the proper clothing.

ENJOYING THE COMPANIONSHIP OF PEOPLE

The people that I met on my seven-month goose hunting trip are numerous. Those that worked in the motels, restaurants, gas stations, retail stores, airports, etc. will never be forgotten. You have to

Glen Sugget from the Manitoba Wildlife Division and the author, with a nice harvest of geese from Kaska Goose Camp on the Hudson Bay.

have a "happy face" for all those days if you are going to keep your sanity and get along with everyone. Getting up before 5 a.m. for almost seven months is no fun. There are days when you wear a "false smile" because you are tired and burnt out.

The people in Manitoba are great. They really identify with the slogan "friendly Manitoba." You might meet a few Canadians that are a little anti-American. However, you can't let that bother you.

The folks in Nebraska are the greatest! Most of them will give you the shirt off of their back. The farmers are most receptive when you ask them if you can use their land to hunt geese on. I still think Nebraska is the best state to hunt in, but hunt in the fall.

The local folks in south Texas were super. Some were a little hard to get close to, but that is true in a lot of areas. There are a few that are still concerned with being around a yankee. However, I got along with everyone and will be back in future years.

GETTING SOME EXERCISE

Nothing could be harder than slogging through the muddy fields in south Texas and Nebraska. These conditions made northern and southern Manitoba seem like a cake walk at a high school dance. Since the fields are too muddy to drive on, particularly in south Texas, all decoys and other gear must be dragged out on Sportsmax sleds. The guides really earn their pay in these conditions!

It's important to be in good physical condition before attempting to hunt in muddy conditions like this. Nothing would be more sad than to see a hunter have a heart attack while goose hunting. I'm sure it has happened. Don't let it happen to you!

THE MEMORIES OF THE TRIP

Memories of a long trip like this are precious. I took over 25 rolls of film with my 35mm camera and used up six tapes on my Canon Hi-8 camcorder. A lot of this will be used for future books and videos on goose hunting. Here are some of the things that I will never forget from each of the areas.

Northern Manitoba

1. Seeing the family of brown bears at Kaska Goose Camp.

2. Seeing the polar bears from the airplane and helicopter at Kaska Goose Camp.

3. Getting to observe the Hudson Bay and seeing the 12 foot waves coming in.

4. Observing York Factory. This is an old trading post that was closed in 1957.

5. Getting to stay at the facilities at Dymond and Kaska and realizing how beautiful they were and how lucky I was to have been at both of them the same year.

6. Getting to meet the great folks at Kaska and Dymond Hunting Lodges.

7. Being able to see the towns of Gillam, Thompson and Churchill, Manitoba. They are beautiful cities.

8. Seeing the Polar Bear Jail in Churchill and the airstrips at Churchill where all the dead geese were laying after colliding with aircraft.

9. Witnessing the great migration of geese that fly north and south along the coast of Hudson Bay.

10. Seeing the tremendous amounts of geese that are harvested at Kaska and Dymond Hunting Camps.

Southern Manitoba

1. The millions of ducks that were flying within 10 miles of my hunting camp.

2. The unusual

Ed Schultz, popular radio and TV personality from Fargo, North Dakota with his son David, and Dennis Hunt. This shoot in southern Manitoba was the best ever for Dennis Hunt. A party of six shot 37 snows, blues and Canadas, as well as five mallards, in 90 minutes.

success of all the hunters who were able to harvest their limits of ducks so effortlessly.

3. The migration of geese that flew over and near to my hunting area.

4. The young calf moose we observed that wandered through our decoy spread.

5. The numerous white-tailed deer we saw in southern Manitoba.

6. The super nice local people from the town and near-by towns where I was hunting for 28 days.

Southern Texas

1. The three million or more geese that were in our vicinity and how easy it was for the hunters from Third Coast Outfitters to get them.

2. The numerous amounts of and the beautiful ducks that are in the south Texas area.

3. The Matagorda, Texas beach and the Gulf of Mexico.

4. John Niemann from Parma, Michigan who was the "bird plucker" extraordinaire and one of the biggest characters I have ever met. John is an avid bow hunter, and harvested a whitefront goose with a bow and

John Niemann from Parma, Michigan, admiring his work and one of his clients.

arrow from 10' in the air after Bobby Hale called the goose in.

5. How great the weather is in November, December and January.

6. The hazards of Texas goose hunting, i.e. fire

Both of these pictures show Bobby Hale and Tainter Wruebel with the 620-pound wild hog that Bobby shot in mid-January of 1997.

ants, water in fields, mud, deep ruts in fields, snakes, wild hogs, alligators etc.

7. The 620-pound wild boar hog that Bobby Hale encountered and killed while out in the field.

8. The 36" rattlesnake that Bobby Hale shot upon returning to his truck.

9. The porpoise that Bobby Hale and I rescued. It was washed onto Matagorda Bay and had been there for

over six hours when we found it and helped it, staying with it for over two hours until it swam away.

10. The duck hunting ordeal where were shooting diver ducks out on the Gulf of Mexico with the weather being 83 degrees and with no shirt on in November.

11. Putting out decoys at 6 a.m. without a shirt on because of the heat and humidity.

12. The wild hogs and the stories about the "macho hog-hunters" who harvest the hogs by using a 12" hog knife.

13. The consistent hunting success of the guides and the clients going out and harvesting 20 to 70, every day of the week, for Third Coast Outfitters.

14. What a great whitefront caller Bobby Hale is.

15. What a great and high profile guide Ben Gregory, from Third Coast Outfitters, is.

16. The 500 yard retrieve that Otter, a golden lab owned by guide Dave Hentosh, made after a snow goose.

A very muddy Texas truck, with some very happy hunters! These South Carolina gunners were guided by Bobby Hale (in the light-colored cap), owner of Third Coast Outfitters.

17. How the geese eat phosphorous and leave goose droppings that glow in the dark, You locate the fields the geese have been in the previous days by looking for the droppings in the fields at 5 a.m.

Nebraska

1. The super migrations of geese flying for hours over our heads, wave after wave.

2. The great weather in February, compared to that of my home state of Minnesota.

3. The number of times you have to get your truck washed so you can see out of the windows.

4. How muddy some of the roads and fields can get.

5. How many law violations I witnessed in 18 days of goose hunting.

6. How many small Canadas and whitefront geese we could have killed if the season was open.

7. How nice the landowners are in Nebraska.

8. The super food and service we got at the Cafe 77 in Beatrice. I want to thank Pam and her staff for opening up two hours early for us.

9. The great Super 8 motel in Beatrice.

10. How an outfitter can charge $275.00 per day to hunt snow geese that are impossible to get without cheating. This guy should have a license to steal.

What Was Learned?

Whenever you go on a goose hunting trip, you will learn something. I always do and it is usually about the geese, my enemy! Hunting in four areas that have different terrains and climates and hunting the same geese from September 1 through March 10 became a learning experience. I learned a lot on that tough and long trip. The things I learned that come to mind are:

1. Learning about the patterns in the different areas.

2. Why some of the geese are easy and some can be so tough to hunt.

3. The positive factors in hunting in the four areas.

4. What the odds are in the different areas.

Do you want to talk about these things? This could make you more knowledgeable on my favorite subject, geese!

THE DIFFERENT PATTERNS IN THE FOUR AREAS

Geese have daily patterns and if you can figure these patterns out, the geese can be predictable. If not, you will be guessing at what they will do tomorrow—and guessing won't get you any birds. You have to know what they are going to do if you are going to stay one step ahead of them and intercept them.

You have to know where they are roosting and what time they leave their roosts each morning. You have to know what they are feeding on, where they are feeding and where they have already fed. And finally, you have to know how much hunting pressure is being put on them. All of this information is important. These are the patterns I found in the different areas.

Northern Manitoba

This was easy! The geese would migrate up and down the coastline and their roosts were in the fresh water pools of water near the coast. Geese

don't drink salt water and they don't roost out on large bodies of water because the water is too rough and they have the tides to contend with. If the geese are in the water and the tide goes out, the predators will get the geese and they know that. The food

Another cart load of snows at Kaska Goose Camp. No Canada geese were killed on this morning because the tide was out and the Canadas were far out on the shoreline. When that happens, the Canada geese won't fly over your blinds which are on the shoreline.

supply was berries and shoots/roots from the grasses out on the eksters. The migration of the geese was along the coastline and that was easy to figure out. Get in a blind along the coast line and wait for them.

Southern Manitoba

The patterns of the geese in this area are also easy. I have hunted this area a lot and have watched them continuously. The same geese come through each season, and they do the same things. They stay in the same roost ponds on the same private lands and go into the same barley fields. They will hit a pea field if there is one available, and will swoop into the corn fields whenever they get harvested. We get

The author and his friends from Minnesota with a nice harvest of geese and ducks in southern Manitoba.

permission to hunt all the barley fields in my hunting area and we have some great results. I watch the geese very closely whenever they feed, and whenever they start feeding in the same field for the second time, I know that they are running out of fields to feed in and will be migrating very shortly.

Southern Texas

The patterns here were easy to figure out. There are over 3 million geese in the area with a limited

Bobby Hale (on the left) from Third Coast Outfitters has figured out the patterns of the geese in south Texas, as this picture shows!

amount of agricultural land in which to feed. The only food available is rice, winter wheat, rye grass, maize and plowed fields. The landowners cut the rice twice and the geese will get into that first. The rice fields are usually void of food by December 15 of each year. Maize is the next thing that the geese will attack, then the winter wheat and the rye grass. The geese live on the marshes which are located on the coastline. They fly north to their feeding fields. If you scout for them you will see the field they are using and should plan to be waiting for them the next day. Most outfitters will flood a field or two to create a roost pond. The geese will use the roost ponds instead of the marshes, making hunting easier. They will leave the roost ponds in the morning and fly a short ways to their feeding field.

Nebraska

Figuring out the geese in Nebraska was a little harder. Many of the geese were migrating in from the south and didn't have a roost pond or place to sleep. They descended into the corn fields because they were hungry and tired. To have success, you had to pick out the likely field they would select to eat in, then put out a quality decoy spread with lots of movement in it. Finding the roost pond was easy because they were staying in flooded corn fields 24 hours a day. Corn is the only food they were interested in eating. They had been in Texas, Oklahoma and Louisiana eating rice, winter wheat, rye grass and maize and they wanted something that would put some body fat on so they could continue their migration northward. Find the flooded corn fields and you found the patterns of the geese in Nebraska.

WHY SOME OF THE GEESE WERE EASY
AND SOME WERE TOUGH TO GET

Some of the geese I hunted in the different areas were easy to decoy and kill, but some were "tough as nails." Let me tell you about them.

Northern Manitoba

The hunting season starts on September 1 on the tundra and the migrating geese had not been hunted since March 10; the immature geese had never seen man before and never heard the sound of a gun. They were easy in northern Manitoba. The food choice was limited and most of the geese were flying over the blinds we were in along the coast line.

Southern Manitoba

The hunting season had been on for 30 days up on the tundra, so some of the migrating geese had been hammered at and were educated. There are always a lot of immature birds that are only three months old and are looking to commit suicide. We always look forward to hunting in southern Manitoba because of this. Geese live by memory and instinct and once you shoot at them and miss, they will remember the sound of a shotgun and the ugly sight of decoys. If you tried to call them in, they will remember that sound also. They learn in a hurry. They have to if they want to live.

Southern Texas

There are a lot of geese in this area and there are a lot of immature birds that escaped the heavy shooting up north. There will be some suicidal geese to kill. However, there are some geese that will not decoy. The only way to get those geese is wait for the heavy fogs to roll in or for the winds to blow 25 miles per hour or stronger. When that happens, the odds are in your favor. Otherwise, the geese are easy in south Texas because there are a lot of geese with a shortage of food. That will add up to success.

Nebraska

The geese that come through here in the spring are desperate to eat corn and build up body fat so they can continue their migration north. You know

Spread those windsocks out and let them flap in the Nebraska winds. They sure worked good in this corn field.

what they will be eating, and there is a shortage of water in Nebraska because there aren't many lakes. The result is that the geese will be in flooded corn fields. Find the corn fields and you will kill geese. They will be easy to get.

THE POSITIVE FACTORS IN HUNTING IN EACH AREA

There are always things that make your goose hunting trip easy, things that you enjoy about the area you're hunting, and things that create good memories. Here are a few things I liked about the areas in which I hunted on this long trip.

Northern Manitoba

You are positive of when the migration will be.
There is no hunting pressure.
You are hunting immature and uneducated geese.
The weather should be ideal.
There is a short distance to your hunting site.

Southern Manitoba

Private land is easy to hunt on.
The weather is ideal for hunting.
You are hunting immature and uneducated geese.
There is only limited hunting pressure on the geese.
The migration is predictable.
You are hunting in the middle of the "duck factory."
There is lots of upland game available.
There is a short distance to your hunting site.

South Texas

The birds are at the end of the migration and have no place to go.

There is a shortage of fields for the birds to feed in, and there are 3 million geese.

There is limited hunting pressure on the geese.

You will be hunting some immature geese that want to commit suicide.

There are ducks, doves, quail and wild hogs to hunt.

The weather is ideal to hunt in with lots of foggy days.

Nebraska

Geese are looking for corn to eat.

There are no lakes for the birds to hide in. They will be in flooded fields.

WHAT ARE YOUR ODDS OF HARVESTING GEESE IN THE FOUR DIFFERENT AREAS?

A goose hunter always wants to know what his chances are before he goes goose hunting. A positive mood will set the tone for a good goose hunt.

Northern Manitoba

You can almost bet on your limits or near limits unless you are shooting badly. I was there and you could almost kill them by throwing rocks at them.

Southern Manitoba

A little harder than northern Manitoba, but still easy. Figure out the patterns and get some quality decoys into a harvested barley field.

South Texas

Get with a good outfitter with a hard-working guide and he will get you some geese. One out of three days should be spectacular. Shooting a white front goose should be a "no brainer." These geese in south Texas are stupid.

Nebraska

Get with an outfitter who knows the territory and will work hard. Don't be afraid of the cold weather in February in Nebraska. The geese are desperate to eat corn and they should be easy to take.

How To Book a Hunt

With private land becoming scarce to hunt on in most states, the only alternative for a goose hunter is to hire a guide through an outfitter. This isn't as expensive as you might think. By the time you are done paying him and you divide the amount paid by the man-hours put in scouting, setting up and taking down the decoys, and driving to and from the hunting site, the man is paid less than $10.00 per hour.

Here are a few things you should know before you book a hunt.

1. The outfitter should be able to supply you with numerous references.

2. The outfitter should be able to provide land for you to hunt on.

3. A competent guide should be provided—one with 20 or more years of hunting experience and 10 years of guiding experience.

4. You should be provided with quality decoys with at least 75% movement.

5. Maximum efforts should be put out by the guide and outfitter.

6. Your accommodations should be above average, and the meals that are served should be good.

To determine if the outfitter will provide these services, call some of the references he provides, and ask them their opinions and also what their hunting success was when they hunted with the outfitter.

After Your Hunt Has Been Booked

After the hunt is booked, the outfitter should supply you with a list of supplies needed for the trip.

Upon arrival at your goose hunting camp, I suggest you do the following.

1. Meet the outfitter and the guide/s.

2. Let the guide know if you are handicapped in any way, i.e. hearing, eyesight, walking, bad back etc. Mention any allergies you have. If you are a diabetic or taking any special medications, tell him about it.

3. Let the guide know he will be working for you, not the other way around. You are paying the fees.

4. Let the guide know the following:
- If you will allow him to shoot or not. Beware of a guide who is a "killer" who will outshoot his clients.
- Find out if he will let you participate in flagging or calling (if you feel qualified to call).

5. Find out the general areas where you will be hunting so you can observe the geese and the terrain. This will get you mentally prepared and set the tone for a quality hunt.

Best Advice

When shopping around to book a hunt to chase some geese, ask the various outfitters a lot of questions. Ask them about their success rates per hunter, per day. If they reply, "We get our limit every day," hang up the phone and call someone else. No goose hunter gets the limit every day of every season, no matter where he goes. It has never happened, it can't happen and it won't happen.

Stay with a small to medium-sized outfitter. If the outfitter takes out more than six hunting parties consistently, you will be a number and not a person.

Geese congregate in large groups and huge flocks, especially snows. They will go to a field where live geese are feeding. They will build up in these fields until they are chased out, or until they eat the field bare. There are only so many fields that will hold geese in each location and I have never seen more than eight. If you go with an outfitter that has 10 to 50 guides that each take out four to six hunters per day, there will be an awful lot of unhappy hunters who will come in with their game straps empty, or with just one bird. It is not possible to find geese to hunt in more than eight fields in a 20-square-mile radius; it just isn't going to happen. The outfitter who has a setup with too many hunters has taken your money and can't get you into any birds.

I am writing this to help you. During this long trip, I have seen a lot of outfitters and heard many comments about various outfitters. My advice to all outfitters: KISS (Keep It Small, Stupid).

If you want to book a hunt at any of the spots mentioned in this book, here are the phone numbers and addresses.

Northern Manitoba
Dymond Hunting Lodge
Stewart or Doug Webber
P.O. Box 304
Churchill, Manitoba R0B 0E0 Canada
Toll-Free: 800-665-0476
204-675-2583

Kaskattama Safari Adventures, Ltd.
(Kaska Goose Camp)
Charlie Taylor
170 Harbison Avenue West
Winnipeg, Manitoba R2L 0A4 Canada
204-667-1611

Southern Manitoba

Dennis Hunt
P.O. Box 131235
St. Paul, Minnesota 55113
612-649-0023 or 218-847-5147

South Texas

Bobby Hale
Third Coast Outfitters
P.O. Box 1351
Bay City, Texas 77404-1351
Toll-Free: 888-TX-GEESE
409-245-3071

Nebraska

Dennis Hunt
P.O. Box 131235
St. Paul, Minnesota 55113
612-649-0023 or 218-847-5147

Summary

To go on a goose hunting trip that carries you over 3,000 miles and lasts over six months could be compared to going through "boot camp" in the Marines. Getting up between 3:30 to 5:00 a.m. daily, setting up decoys, taking down decoys, scouting and watching geese constantly could put you on the edge of insanity. Many times you have the "burnt out syndrome" and want to quit goose hunting and sell your guns. To keep going every day takes a man who is mentally and physically tough and a little bit "nuts." I want to thank God for bringing me back alive.

I hope this book will help you improve your goose hunting. If I can be of any help in any way, be sure to call or write:

Dennis Hunt
P.O. Box 131235
St. Paul, Minnesota 55113
612-649-0023 or 218-847-5147

I hope to see you in one of these areas in the future. Be careful and don't break the law. I hope you get some opportunities to shoot your gun. That is what hunting is all about.

Previous Books by Dennis Hunt

Dennis Hunt is the author of three previous books on goose hunting: *The Science of Snow Goose Hunting, Goose Hunting: Improving Your Skills,* and *Out-Finessing The Geese.* They are available at selected sporting-goods stores and bookstores, and can also be purchased directly from Dennis Hunt for $19,95 each (U.S. postage included). Send a check or Visa card number to Dennis Hunt, P.O. Box 131235, St. Paul, Minnesota 55113.

Dennis Hunt also has produced a beautiful color video entitled "The Science of Goose Hunting: Improving Your Skills," which is available for $19.95.

Seminars

Dennis Hunt gives goose-hunting seminars at many sports shows across the country. Check the listings at your next local sports show; if Dennis is not one of the featured speakers, let the show management know that you'd like to see him at a seminar!

Hunting Equipment Featured In This Book

All the hunting merchandise mentioned in this book can be purchased at most sporting goods stores, or through Dennis Hunt. Call or write Dennis Hunt for more information on any of these products.

The Science of
Snow Goose Hunting

*By Bob Guist
as told by Dennis Hunt*

**Goose Hunting:
Improving Your Skills**

By Dennis Hunt

**Out-Finessing
The Geese**

By Dennis Hunt

Dennis Hunt
The Science of
Goose Hunting:

Improving Your Skills

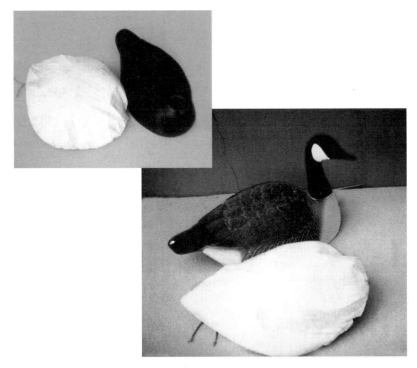

The Convertadecoy Sleeve

Designed by Dennis Hunt and manufactured by North Wind Decoy Co., the Convertadecoy Sleeve is a two-sided piece of tough tyvek material. One side is white and the other side is brown. The Convertadecoy Sleeve fits over all shell, full body or silhouette decoys. It is held tight with a drawstring. It can be used to convert a white shell into a Canada, blue or whitefront goose by putting the brown side of the Convertadecoy Sleeve over the white decoy. It also eliminates repainting of decoys, prevents frost from getting on the decoy and takes up almost no space. Convertadecoy Sleeve owners can slit the sleeve to create movement. Cost is $24.95 per dozen, plus $3 shipping and handling. Minnesota residents add 6.5% sales tax. Available from Dennis Hunt, P.O. Box 131235, St. Paul MN 55113. Phone (612) 649-0023, fax (612) 644-3653. Call with Visa or send check.